Your First Dog:
What to Expect

Your First Dog:
What to Expect

Timothy Falcon Crack
*PhD (MIT), MCom, PGDipCom,
BSc (HONS 1st Class), IMC*

©2025 TIMOTHY FALCON CRACK

All rights reserved worldwide. No part of this book may be reproduced, stored in a retrieval system, or transmitted in any form or by any means, electronic, mechanical, photocopying, recording, or otherwise, without the prior written permission of the author.

Warning: The author accepts no liability in any event including (without limitation) negligence for any damages or loss of any kind, including (without limitation) direct, indirect, incidental, special or consequential damages, expenses or losses arising out of, or in connection with, your use or inability to use the information in this book.

Published by: Timothy Falcon Crack, P.O. Box 6385, Dunedin North, Dunedin 9059, New Zealand.

Front cover image: Hazel the Chocolate Labrador, aged nine months. Rear cover image: Hazel the Chocolate Labrador, aged four years.

First edition, Second Printing, August 2025.
ISBN: 978-1-0670583-1-9

Typeset by the author.
timcrack@alum.mit.edu

Contents

Preface	vii
1 Introduction	1
2 First Things First	3
3 We Wish We Had Known	23
4 Unpleasant Surprises	35
5 Other Surprises	59
6 We Learned the Hard Way	105
7 Dog Ownership Pros & Cons	135
7.1 Pros of Dog Ownership	135
7.2 Cons of Dog Ownership	137

CONTENTS

7.3	Dog Ownership Checklist	141
7.4	Final Words 🐾	142

References   145

Index   147

Preface

What is it like to own your first dog? We list the many surprises that we faced with our first dog, Hazel. We tell you what we wish we had known in advance, what we would do differently next time, and what we learned the hard way. We finish with general pros and cons of dog ownership.

We did a lot of dog research before bringing Hazel into our family. Nevertheless, we still faced a constant barrage of surprises that no book, web site, or other dog owner had prepared us for. Given our prior research, why did we face so many surprises?

We think the problem is that much of the advice we took was from "experts." The experts likely grew up with dogs and/or had multiple dogs over their lifetimes. The shock of bringing a first dog into their family was something that either they never knew

PREFACE

(because their parents had handled any problems when they were children) or it was something they had long since forgotten about.

We are not experts, but ordinary people, and we have done our best here to tell you what to expect with your first dog. My family and I wish you the best of success with your own first-dog adventure.

Feedback

I invite you to send me e-mails with queries, corrections, and constructive criticism. If you have some gem of an idea that you think will add value, please let me know! I revise my books frequently, and I will be happy to include any contribution that adds value, no matter how small. If I use your material, I will thank you in the next edition.

If this book helps you, please leave a positive review on www.Amazon.com. Search for this book on Amazon's Web site and click on the box labeled, "Write a customer review." Thank you!

timcrack@alum.mit.edu

Chapter 1

Introduction

Our goal is to help you to decide whether to bring a first dog into your family. We try to meet this goal in two ways. First, we give advice on first-dog ownership, based on our first four years with our first dog. Second, we give more than 100 brief accounts of experiences with our first dog, many of which contained surprises for us. Many of these accounts relay seemingly disconnected vignettes, but they are connected via the common thread of dog ownership. We hope that the collection as a whole paints an accurate, if somewhat gnarly, picture of dog ownership.

We had no experience at all with dogs before we

CHAPTER 1. INTRODUCTION

brought Hazel (an eight-week old pure-bred Chocolate English Labrador puppy) into our family. Although we had no prior experience, I think that we have succeeded in raising a very happy healthy dog.

Hazel is a well-socialized dog, likes almost everybody, is gentle with children and old people, and is empathetic. Achieving this outcome has, however, taken considerable time, effort, and money, and we are surprised at the damage to our home, our garden, our possessions, and our bodies.

We did lots of research before we even decided to own a dog, and since bringing Hazel into our family we have had four years of "on-the-job training" (sometimes a baptism by fire). It took many trial-and-error experiments to see what worked for us and what worked for Hazel.

Our first-dog experience has been challenging and rewarding in equal measures. If you have never had a dog in the family, your experience may be very different from what you are expecting; it has been in our case.

We hope that our advice and our stories bring the first-dog experience to life for you and help you to make an informed decision about bringing a dog into your family, or not.

Chapter 2

First Things First

Do you think you have room in your life for a dog companion? Have you always wanted a dog? Is a child begging you for a puppy? How do you decide whether to get a dog, and if so, which breed?

The very first thing you should do is to read as much as you possibly can about what it is like to have a dog in your life. Be sure to also talk to people you know with dogs. Visit a dog owner in their house and go for dog walks with them, to the park or beach, etc. Most dog owners will be happy to let you do that. Getting a dog is a big commitment, and not something to take lightly. If possible, go to a park where there are lots of dogs, and see how

CHAPTER 2. FIRST THINGS FIRST

different they are from each other. Talk to owners of different breeds and ask questions: What is the best thing about owning your dog? What is the worst thing about owning your dog? Is your dog always this aggressive? Why does your dog bark non-stop? Does your dog always jump up on people? Etc.

We started off by reading as much as we could about puppy training and dog training, both in books and on web sites. Then, we asked a dog trainer for advice on picking a breed for our family. She did not recommend a particular breed for us, but she told us the following two things:

- First, get a pure breed (e.g., Labrador), not a mixed breed (e.g., Labradoodle, etc.). She had seen lots of behavioral and physical issues in mixed breeds over the years. Behavioral issues can occur because although different breeds have distinct behaviors, a mixed-breed dog does not know how to behave, and it can give confusing signals to other dogs, and to humans. Physical issues can occur because the body shapes of most dog breeds are different (that is one reason why we recognize them as distinct breeds when we see them). Once you start mixing breeds, however, the various body parts do not necessarily fit together properly, leading to joint issues.

- Second, use an accredited breeder who has proof of pedigree. This is to avoid health and behavioral problems. The dog trainer said it often costs the same as buying a puppy from a non-accredited stranger online. From what we have observed in over four years of meeting other dogs when we are out with our dog, this has turned out to be very good advice.

We chose a pure-bred English Labrador because we thought that this breed would suit our family: Friendly, intelligent, able to be trained, good with old people and children, and large enough to deter bad people if my wife or daughter is walking the dog by themselves.

We assumed initially that we would get a Golden Labrador. We even put down a $150 deposit on a Golden Labrador we saw for sale online. (Note: All prices quoted in this book are expressed in U.S. dollars.) Ultimately, however, we decided it was safer to go to an accredited breeder, and the litter we saw there had a lovely dark Chocolate English Labrador puppy. We chose her, and we named her Hazel. She cost $1,500. We lost the deposit on the Golden Labrador, which we did not regret.

We considered other breeds. For example, if you want an "easy" dog that does not shed, is quiet

CHAPTER 2. FIRST THINGS FIRST

and well behaved, sleeps a lot, likes being at home, loves people, and does not need a lot of walking, we think that a French Bulldog is a good option. They are, of course, extremely popular for these reasons, and very expensive. However, I do not think that they are large enough or fierce enough to deter people with bad intent. So, that was a strike against the breed in my eyes; I wanted something bigger—something that goes **"WOOF!"**, not something that goes *"yap."*

What about a Border Collie? We live in New Zealand now, and given New Zealand's farming backbone, we see many Border Collies around, often at work herding sheep. They are highly intelligent, cute puppies, widely available, and affordable, but they require a lot of walking and training, or they get bored easily. They are a very high-maintenance dog, really meant to be a working farm dog. So, we think you should avoid Border Collies unless you have a lot of time and energy. If you finish reading this book, and think that a Labrador requires more time and energy than you possess, then you certainly should not consider a Border Collie, which we think requires an order of magnitude more of your time.

Now that we have a dog, we meet and talk to

100 times as many dogs and dog owners as we used to. That was a surprise at first, but it is partly explained by us going to places where dog owners go, at times when they go there, so that Hazel can have mini play dates. It is also partly explained by most other dogs out on walks stopping to say hello to Hazel in the street; the dogs say hello and the dog owners say hello.

After meeting many hundreds and hundreds of dogs, our advice is that you not get a "rescue dog." Leave them to people who are *very* experienced with dogs and willing to cope with and work on their many behavioral issues. Ninety-five percent of rescue dogs we meet (my wife says 99%) have ongoing issues with aggression, lack of socialization, etc. Their owners seem to be almost uniformly disappointed with their new doggy family member. We think that rescue dogs are not for first-time dog owners.

We live in a small city, of about 50,000 households (130,000 persons). I was surprised to find that there are 18,500 dogs registered with our City Council. Many dog owners have more than one dog. So, we guess that about one house in five has a dog living there; that is also the ratio we see on our street.

CHAPTER 2. FIRST THINGS FIRST

We walk Hazel twice a day. In total, it averages about 90–120 minutes each day, but it is often more. It is very time consuming and uses lots of energy. Any good vet/trainer will tell you that a large dog like a Labrador needs at least 90 minutes of exercise per day (preferably split in two) for health and good behavior. Some breeds, like Border Collies, may need more exercise than this, but smaller dogs, like a French Bulldog, may need much less.

You must consider the time and exercise needed (and your physical fitness, or desired physical fitness) before choosing a dog. Let me add that I do not believe that I have ever met an obese dog owner. Even overweight dog owners are rare. So much exercise is required that unfit people either do not get a dog in the first place, or if they do get one, they are not taking it out for much exercise (and it is likely unhappy about that).

Dog walks will be very short at first, as your puppy's bones are still growing; a young puppy may not even be able to walk up or down stairs. Your walks become very long later when your dog has grown. Ask yourself whether you are physically fit enough to walk a dog for 90 minutes or more every day, and whether you are physically strong enough (i.e., both upper body strength and leg strength) to handle a medium- to large-sized dog that suddenly lunges at something (or at some animal). Answers to these questions will help you to determine whether you want a dog, and which breed that might be. Ask a neighbor on your street who has a dog to let you walk their dog, likely with them as a chaperone; if you end up getting pulled over and dragged 20 paces on your backside in the park, or you get pulled backwards through a hedge, then maybe that dog is too big for you.

There are many different dog training methods, not one "correct" method. We ended up choosing a method recommended by animal behaviorists (i.e., scientists) that emphasizes positive reinforcement. This seems to be the most modern, logical and proven method. It is different from the old-fashioned methods (based on tradition) that include negative reinforcement (which many people still teach/use with varying success). The bottom line is that we withhold affection or attention or treats for *bad* behavior (e.g., turning our back on Hazel and ignoring her), but we give lots of praise, affection, attention, and treats for *good* behavior. This has been extremely successful; we discuss this in more detail later.

Given our successful experiences, the dog train-

CHAPTER 2. FIRST THINGS FIRST

ing book we recommend is "*Total Recall*" by Pippa Mattinson, an animal behaviorist from England. She also runs a website called "The Labrador Site" (`www.TheLabradorSite.com`).

We saw "puppy classes" advertised in our town. We tried them out, and found that they were mostly about socializing your puppy with other dogs and people (which is very important). We did get some generic dog training advice, but nothing special. Some of these classes gave some advice we thought was bad. There may be waiting lists for these classes. So, it is best to sign up early, before you even get a dog.

A senior colleague, who had had many dogs, said that your new dog wants to please you, but does not know how. Thus, learning how to communicate (both ways) is really important. This takes time and effort. I fear, however, that many people do not have the time and do not make the effort, leading to an unhappy relationship. That is partly why we see so many unhappy dogs and so many unhappy dog owners.

So far, we have taught Hazel more than 60 verbal commands or names of things. I rarely hear other dog owners using such a wide variety of commands with such success. Some other dog owners are surprised when Hazel reacts to some of my commands (e.g., "look both ways" before we cross the railway lines, or a silent hand-signal countdown 3-2-1-0 from a distance before running to get a ball). (Hazel also knows the names of about 10 human friends/neighbors and at least 20 dog friends.)

Most of what we taught Hazel are verbal commands using English words that you would recognize. About 10% of these verbal commands are, however, not English words, but a foreign phrase or just a vocal noise. For example, a coughed "ahem!" before I open a door or cross a street means Hazel has to sit before being allowed to proceed, a "uh, uh, uuuh!" means no, do not do it, a "did, dot" clucking sound with the tongue means come here for a piece of kibble (i.e., her regular hard dime-sized dog food). I often use that last command when I am walking Hazel and I notice that her lead is getting tight (because she is pulling ahead), when the goal is for it to be slack (with her walking at my side).

It is important to not mix up commands. For example, to Hazel "down" means get down on your belly, but I accidentally said "down" when she put her feet on the kitchen counter, which confused her. Now I am careful to say "off" instead in that case,

CHAPTER 2. FIRST THINGS FIRST

to avoid confusion.

We taught Hazel about a half-dozen silent commands. These include hand signals (for come, sit, stay, quiet, "no more food," and countdowns with fingers) and also lead signals (e.g., a gentle tug on the lead when stopping at a street corner means to sit, a repeated gentle tug of the upper lead to one side when walking on a sidewalk downtown means move over to make room for an oncoming pedestrian, and moving both leads to the left or right means go to the left or the right—like using reins on a horse). (Note: We use a double-lead two-point harness; discussed later.) We have also done some successful whistle training for recall (i.e., coming back to you when off-lead), but that has to be frequently reinforced with high-value treats (e.g., fresh boiled chicken, bacon treats) or her skills fade quickly.

There is a forward-looking element to some of these commands that we were initially unaware of. For example, my wife was walking Hazel at the park and came upon an elderly gentleman with his 13-year-old Golden Retriever. His dog had suddenly gone completely deaf. He was trying to teach it hand commands, but, believe it or not, it really is difficult to teach an old dog new tricks. Other old dogs we know are deaf and blind, or nearly so. In those cases, a silent command or a lead command could be very useful. So, we strongly recommend that you start training on vocabulary and silent commands (hand signals and lead signals) from Day 1.

Do not expect your dog to generalize. That is, you may have to teach your dog to sit at home, sit at the park, sit at a street corner downtown, and sit at the beach, etc. Dogs do tend to view training with a narrow, almost autistic focus. This surprised me at first, and patience was a key to success.

I was very surprised that training Hazel sometimes involves giving her rewards for *doing nothing*. For example, if she sits by the kitchen entrance making plaintive "I want what you are cooking sounds" howling or barking and you give her attention by asking her to be quiet, then she knows that making that noise in that circumstance in the future yields attention—and she loves attention. If, however, you gently say "shuuush, quiet puppy," with a finger to your lips, and then wait for silence and then give a reward only if she is actually quiet for five to ten seconds, saying "good quiet puppy," then that is different. Then, when she sits there quietly in future doing *nothing*, you can say "good

CHAPTER 2. FIRST THINGS FIRST

quiet puppy" with a finger to your lips and a gentle "shuuush" and give her a reward for doing nothing. The more we do this, the more Hazel learns that being quiet is the desired behavior in that circumstance. This training has also proved useful in physical confrontation situations in the street, as described later.

Different breeds have different behaviors. Some dogs bark a lot: in the house, in the garden, when on a lead in the street, etc. Some dogs (e.g., Labradors) eat everything. Some dogs (e.g., Greyhounds) have awful recall (i.e., refusing to come back when you call). Some dogs love humans, but do not like other dogs. Some dogs (e.g., Border Collies) can be quite indifferent to humans or dogs outside their family. Some dogs (e.g., German Shepards) are very difficult to train. You might choose a Poodle because they do not shed, only to find that you have to pay to take it to the groomer all the time. Also, every Poodle (or Poodle-cross) I have met has been ill-tempered. Personally, I would rather have a friendly dog that sheds than an ill-tempered Poodle. We bump into many breeds and situations where the owners are clearly disappointed or frustrated that their dog did not meet their expectations.

We have never taken Hazel to a groomer, because there is nothing to groom. So, we have no personal experience with that. I was surprised, however, that a neighborhood dog owner with a Golden Retriever said that he could not find a groomer in the city who could see his dog in the next three months. He had just booked his dog three months in advance for grooming. His dog looked quite shaggy and unkempt.

What about spaying females, heats, and neutering males? This is a complicated decision, and best advice differs with sex and with breed. Two studies out of the University of California Davis give detailed suggestions, based on sex and breed. Hart *et al* (2020) discuss 35 breeds and Hart *et al* (2024) discuss an additional five breeds, and include a table covering all 40 breeds mentioned in the two studies. (References appear at the end of this book.) In general, the earlier you spay or neuter, the more likely that subsequent bone/joint issues develop, and the later you spay or neuter the more likely that subsequent cancers develop. Size is also an important factor, with most smaller dogs being less likely to suffer from joint disorders and cancers. So, there is a weighing up of competing risk factors and competing protective factors.

CHAPTER 2. FIRST THINGS FIRST

We concluded that many of the protective factors could be achieved by spaying Hazel (a female Labrador) just after nine months—though Hart *et al* (2020) suggest waiting until 12 months. We tilted towards nine months so that we did not have to suffer through any heats. (We do, however, see people walking their dogs in heat, against our city's dog bylaws.) Interestingly, Hart *et al* (2020) recommend that female Golden Retrievers not be spayed at all, even though we think of them as being quite similar to Labradors.

Let me now discuss money for 10 paragraphs. The basic message is that you must be prepared to spend a lot of money on your dog because there is no way to care properly for your dog cheaply.

You may need to factor in the cost of some new furniture. For example, in advance of bringing a dog into our house, we worried about our cat (and rightfully so, because our cat and Hazel did not mix for the first year because Hazel just wanted to get the cat). We bought a big new piece of furniture for our hallway, so that we could feed the cat at an elevated level (four feet off the ground). We can now leave a bowl of cat food there for the cat to graze upon, which otherwise Hazel would just eat instantly. I also used a jig-saw to fabricate a very extended waist-high semi-circular wooden shelf that slots into a corner bookshelf. Now, the cat has a place to sit in the living room where Hazel can not get her. It has turned out to have many other uses. For example, my wife uses it as a stand-up desk sometimes.

I listened to an episode of the *Ramsey Show* (a popular U.S. talk-radio show, where the hosts discuss getting out of debt, building wealth, careers, etc.). One day they were discussing people who cannot afford to buy a dog and instead finance their dogs. That is, they borrow money to buy their dog and then have a monthly payment on their dog, including interest on the borrowed money. Unlike a car loan, I think it must be an unsecured loan (i.e., a loan that is not tied to a specific item of valuable collateral). So, the interest rate is likely comparable to that on a credit card. I had never heard of anyone financing a dog; I was horrified.

If you do not have enough money to pay for your dog in cash, then you should not buy a dog. Buying a dog using borrowed money is completely ridiculous. Similarly, if you do not have enough money set aside in the bank for dog emergencies (or if you cannot afford pet insurance), then you should not buy a dog.

CHAPTER 2. FIRST THINGS FIRST

Here are several other examples of surprise costs: Our neighbor's dog ate some dry seaweed which caused an internal blockage. The neighbors paid $550 in vet bills to get the dog examined; there was no surgery. On another day, I met a couple walking a young Labrador puppy. It looked about five or six months old. They said that in its puppy rambunctiousness it had fallen down stairs in their house and got a "spiral fracture" of its fibula. It had to be treated in a different city, 250 miles away. It ended up costing them $4,800. My opinion is that you should not own a dog unless you have a spare $1,000+ on hand for emergencies, or unless you have pet insurance.

Out of curiosity, I contacted a vet-related lender who said I could borrow money for vet bills. They said that the interest rate is determined by my credit score and that "On a loan of $3,000 over two years the weekly payment would be around $35—this is based on an interest rate of 19.95% plus with six months interest free (if you qualify for this)." (Note: Those interest payments amount to an extra $640 in interest over and above the amount borrowed.) There are probably also "establishment fees" to set the loan up in the first place.

The financial costs of dog ownership can be awful. You have to pay for your dog, pay for food, pay for regular vet bills, buy toys, buy bedding, buy and install protection (e.g., wire netting for tree trunks, covers for wires in the house, matting for gravel, matting for vegetable patches, etc.). We heard horror stories about dogs getting their stomachs pumped after gorging themselves on dog food that was left in reach. So, we bought a big sturdy plastic garbage can with a locking lid to keep her 30-pound (15kg) bag of dog food in. Then there is city registration, training costs, leads, collar, implanted identification chip, etc. It quickly adds up to many thousands of dollars—and those are *after-tax* dollars. A bag of food for our adult Labrador is close to $120 every seven weeks. That is about $900 a year, just for basic food. We are also surprised at the cost (and often the unavailability) of the dog poo bags we use every day; they arrive in our supermarket and sell out almost immediately.

The financial costs of dog ownership are not just direct costs. There are also large indirect "opportunity costs." For example, walking a dog twice a day is very disruptive to a work-from-home schedule. You lose out on the income that you might have earned, and you do so while paying for the basic day-to-day costs of operating a dog. Consider

CHAPTER 2. FIRST THINGS FIRST

losing two hours per day of household income. At the U.S. Federal minimum wage ($7.25 per hour; DOL [2025]), that amounts to a $5,000 opportunity cost per year. If your dog lives ten years, then that is a $50,000 pre-tax opportunity cost, ignoring the time value of money. At the average U.S. wage per hour ($36.30 per hour in June 2025; BLS [2025]), the opportunity cost is exactly five times that: $250,000. I am a textbook author. For all that time and money, I could have written a new textbook and earned enough money to put an extension on my house. In fact, I could have written a new textbook in my new extension!

The bottom line on the financial front is that a dog is a *luxury*. So, before buying a dog, you must be sure that you understand the impact of dog ownership on your monthly budget. If you cannot afford to pay cash up front for your dog, or if you cannot afford a couple of hundred dollars a month in basic expenses (e.g., food, vet bills, and accessories), or if you cannot set aside at least a thousand dollars as an emergency fund (or $50–$100 per month for pet insurance), then, unfortunately, you cannot afford a dog in your life at this time.

We recommend that you have a support network in place in advance of getting a dog. That way, if an emergency comes up (e.g., a family member is hospitalized), you will have someone lined up who can take in your dog at short notice. Ideally, it will be someone with experience with dogs, and someone that your dog knows. In our case, we have family in town and also a local dog sitter we have used several times who might take her in at short notice. In a very brief emergency, Hazel knows four neighbors, who all love her and would, we think take her for an afternoon, if needed.

I am semi-retired, my wife is a homemaker, and we still have a teenager at home. We think that we care for our dog Hazel well. She seems happy and well adjusted, and most people she meets seem to really like her. If, however, one or both of us were still working full time, I do not think it would be possible at all for us to have Hazel as a pet, and for her to be as happy and well-adjusted and well-socialized as she seems to be. At least, it would not be possible without also paying for a dog walker to come to our house every day to walk Hazel for us. We feel, however, that bringing in that other person would weaken our bond with Hazel and confuse her to some extent. Maybe if Hazel were some other breed that does not care as much about human companionship, or does not need as much exercise, it

CHAPTER 2. FIRST THINGS FIRST

would be a different story.

Let us close this chapter by saying that you have to be sure to do enough research to allow you to choose a dog breed that fits into your work/life schedule. If not, your dog may be less than fully happy (for 10+ years) and you will be frustrated by the experience (for 10+ years). You do not want what should be a blessing to become a curse. It would be heartbreaking (and confusing to the dog) to have to take your family pet to the pound, hoping that someone else will adopt him or her because you are not able to live up to your dog's needs.

Chapter 3

We Wish We Had Known

There are many other things that we wish we had known in advance. Some of these might even have stopped us bringing a dog into the family.

One day at the dog park my wife met a young man with a four-month-old baby and a one-year-old dog. He told my wife that he had found raising a puppy to be harder than taking care of his newborn baby. In his words, "Both need constant care and attention, but at least a baby wears a diaper (nappy) and does not run around peeing everywhere and chewing the furniture!" Though it has

CHAPTER 3. WE WISH WE HAD KNOWN

been a decade and a half since we had a newborn baby in the house, my wife was inclined to agree with him. At least, given the phenomenal growth rate with a puppy, the intense care-giving stage does not last quite as long as it does with a baby.

Be prepared for major sleep deprivation for the first several months with your puppy. We think it is rare (and lucky) to get a dog that instantly sleeps through the night, just as it is with human babies. Someone had to get up every two hours to take Hazel outside when she was a little puppy. Again, it was like having a new baby in the house.

Also be prepared for the "puppy blues" (i.e., the regret that you got a puppy) while you are in this stage; it should pass after a few months.

Hazel pooed, peed, and puked in the house on occasion for the first few months. It was like having a newborn baby in the house. You can buy absorbent mats to put down, along with newspaper, but it is still an awful mess to clean up.

Hazel damaged wooden furniture by chewing on it. Chair legs, table legs, etc. She stopped after a few months.

Hazel damaged our woolen carpet by digging with the claws on her big flipper feet. There is no point replacing it until your dog is older, so you may be stuck with wrecked carpet for a year or more.

Hazel damaged curtains over our back door by rubbing against them going in and out of house. Her dark coat has natural oils, which have damaged the material. We doubt that dry-cleaning will fix this damage.

Hazel damaged dozens of plants/trees in the garden, including killing old ones we spent 15+ years nurturing. She destroyed them completely in minutes. Hazel damaged grass in the garden by peeing on it and killing it, and by digging holes in it. Four years on, and the grass is still not recovered. She even damaged our footpath and brick pavers in the garden by digging at them.

Hazel also barks suddenly sometimes, at possums/hedgehogs in the garden, late at night, disturbing the neighbors.

Hazel sheds fur in the house. It gets everywhere. No matter how often we wash and brush her to collect fur, it still keeps appearing in the house, on floors, furniture, tables, clothes, etc. We bought an expensive vacuum cleaner made for this purpose, which helps, mostly. It has a cylindrical brush roller than agitates the carpet and picks up pet fur, but at the risk of damaging the carpet a little.

I was surprised that the lint filter of the clothes

CHAPTER 3. WE WISH WE HAD KNOWN

drying machine gets full of dog fur, even when the clothes or blankets coming out of the clothes washing machine look perfectly clean. Drying your clothes on the washing line instead does not get the fur off. (We did a test where we line-dried a blanket almost to completion and then machine dried it, and the lint filter was still full of fur.)

Hazel smells like a dog, even when freshly washed and dried off. Some people like the smell, but some people do not. Having a dog in your house makes rooms, and your house in general, smell like a dog. There is the old English joke: Man 1: "I say, I say, I say, my dog's got no nose." Man 2: "How does he smell?" Man 1: "Awful!"

Our dog training (lead walking, recall, obedience, etc.) was intense for the first year. After that, we have had to maintain her training with daily refresher sessions; refreshing learned skills is much easier than the original training was.

The first year can feel like very hard work because puppies are super hyperactive, but Hazel, like most dogs, began to settle down after the first year or two, and to become more relaxed and well behaved. I am not sure that we would have gotten Hazel if we had known in advance about the intense effort required over that first year.

Not everyone can handle having a dog in their house seven days a week, because it is such hard work. We met a lady walking her little dog at our Esplanade who said that one day a week, she puts her dog into a doggy day care, just so that she gets some respite. We also met a man at our local park with a lovely Chocolate Labrador who said he does the same thing. Note that this doggy day-care has cost implications on top of the need-for-respite implications.

I was surprised to find that when I walk down the street, Hazel always wants to walk against the fence line or building wall. That is, she does not want to walk on the side of the sidewalk where the road is. I think that it is because the fence line is where the good smells are. It is where other dogs have left their markings. (She is "reading her pee-mail" as one passerby quipped.)

I almost always have Hazel walk on my right-hand side. In my city, however, people almost always walk on the left-hand side of the sidewalk (unless they are foreigners or tourists). We used to even have signs up in the middle of the sidewalk in our central city saying "keep left," with an arrow pointing left. So, Hazel wanting to walk on my right and wanting to walk along the fence line can create some

CHAPTER 3. WE WISH WE HAD KNOWN

confrontations. I do try to pull her over to the left-hand-side of the sidewalk when people are coming, but some folks just move out of the way when they see me coming with a decent-sized dog, and then I stay on the right. With hindsight, given the local mores, perhaps I should have trained Hazel to walk on my left-hand side, so that she could get access to the good smells without disrupting foot traffic.

When I do pull Hazel over to the left-hand-side of the sidewalk, I have to be careful, because the instant the oncoming walkers pass by, she tries to pull back over to the right. She wants to do it so quickly that she would brush against the backs of their legs, almost tripping them over. So, I now hold on to her extra tightly until passersby are a few feet past us, otherwise it looks for all the world like she is trying to attack their feet.

I have heard it said that "golf is a good walk spoiled." I was surprised to find this also to be true of walking a dog. Hazel loves to smell everything when she walks. This means that although walking to work by myself takes only 35 minutes without Hazel, it takes a full 65 minutes with her. It is frustrating (and not good exercise) to have to keep stopping suddenly. If, however, I refuse to let Hazel smell things, then she is very unhappy, because smelling things is her great joy; she lives in (and lives for) a world of smells.

If you are fit and you exercise a lot and you have a busy schedule, then you may find it very frustrating to take a dog for a walk because of stopping to sniff things for a loooong time every 20 paces. It is so frustrating to have to keep stopping. It nullifies some aspects of the exercise, upsets your rhythm, takes extra time, and can mean that you arrive late at your destination. Also, a dog's sudden stops can be jarring to your writs, elbows, shoulders, lower back and knees.

I have been jogging for more than 40 years. I tried to jog with Hazel, but she will not jog more than 20 paces unless she has an obvious goal ahead of her (e.g., the little park in town that often has pigeons) or unless she is at the beach. She is simply not built for it. She is the wrong breed for running. She does, however, love to swim; ironically, I cannot swim. She has, however, been very protective of my son in the water when he is swimming.

When I am out and about with Hazel, there is a constant worry that she might bite a child or an old person. Hazel has a lovely nature and is very calm with children and old people, but if a child does something unpredictable, like suddenly shriek-

CHAPTER 3. WE WISH WE HAD KNOWN

ing or suddenly grabbing Hazel etc., Hazel might get scared and defend herself. This risk is a constant stress when out walking. When we stop to talk to people, I often hold her lead very tightly. If small children are there, I often kneel down and put my arm around Hazel, or I hold her harness, or I hold her collar or her head, to ensure that I have full physical control over her.

A young man with a clear intellectual disability knelt down to pat Hazel. Lots of people want to pat Hazel, including many disabled people. So, I thought little of it. I was surprised, however, when he started to hug her and then his hug got tighter and tighter, like she was a big stuffed furry toy dog. Hazel started to look confused and distressed, looking from him to me and back several times, and she started to squirm to get away from him. I was worried that she would get aggressive and bite him in self defense. I pulled her away from his grip before anything bad could happen; I will not let that happen again.

Some things humans eat are poison/toxic to dogs: chocolate, macadamia nuts, xylitol, caffeine, and raisins/sultanas (though there is some disagreement between sources on raisins/sultanas). Some foods just make dogs sick: onions/garlic, pits from fruit (e.g., apples, apricots). It is a constant worry when baking, etc. It is also a worry when walking in the street; I often have to suddenly grab Hazel and open her jaws to get her to drop a chocolate-chip cookie or a piece of cake or a chicken bone that she lunged at and picked up in the street.

Hazel can be restless at night if she ate something inappropriate during the day (gravel, tree bark, sticks, stones, seaweed, chewy/stretchy rotting animal carcass, dog poo, horse poo, etc.). This disrupts our sleep and may require us to clean up a vomit mess at 2AM or 3AM.

Hazel was acting oddly on a recent walk, even after doing a big healthy poo in the park and lots of pees. We walked home on city streets, with her stopping much more than usual, and several times refusing to move on. Then she surprised me with a second poo, only when this one hit the sidewalk, it made the same sound that you would hear if you dropped a carpenter's pencil onto cement; it was 95% made up of sticks and bits of wood. After that, she felt much better and was her usual self.

Finally, for this chapter, sometimes you may notice your dog licking its butt excessively and/or scooting its butt across the carpet. This may signal that you need to express your dog's anal glands.

CHAPTER 3. WE WISH WE HAD KNOWN

Yes, the advice in the next five paragraphs is going to be gross.

In Hazel's case, she also gets restless, jumpy, and does not sleep well when she has this problem brewing. These glands (also called "anal sacs") are grape-sized/shaped and located internally beside the anus. They are at about four o'clock and eight o'clock relative to, and a quarter-finger length inside, the dog's anus. They contain a foul-smelling thick liquid. If the glands function normally, they express fluid whenever the dog poos, and the fluid marks their poo as a means of communication to other dogs. It can also be expressed in times of great stress (which could be one reason why Hazel gets nervous at the vet, smelling other dogs' secretions). Some dogs will never have a problem. Hazel has a problem, genetically we think, on her left-side only, and we have to help her out about once every three or four weeks.

If Hazel has not chewed enough sticks lately (which helps to stimulate gland secretion when they pass by) the glands can get backed up. Then you have to squeeze them (with or without a finger inserted) in order for them to release excess fluid. This fluid can squirt three to six feet (one or two metres) and is amazingly foul smelling.

As a father to young children, I changed at least 500 poopy diapers (nappies). The smell from Hazel's anal gland fluid is comparable to that coming from the worst diaper I ever smelled after a child had been awfully unwell and produced something not even recognizable as a poo. We jokingly referred to it as "fish-butt Friday" after doing it on a Friday, but now we cannot use the expression "fish-butt" without Hazel looking alarmed, thinking that she will have to go outside for her treatment.

The first time I expressed Hazel's anal glands I wore only surgical gloves, and the smell stayed with me for many hours; I just kept smelling it over and over up my nose all day, perhaps as some sort of nasal hallucination (a so-called "phantosmia"); that has happened more than once. Sometimes I wear a high-level mask, a rain coat that is easy to clean, surgical gloves and safety glasses to do this. Other times, I wear just the gloves and take the risk.

I put Vaseline on a gloved fingertip and in that same hand I hold a folded paper towel, to try to catch the squirting liquid. Afterwards, I wash the dog's butt/tail/hind area with warm water and dog shampoo (this is the only time I use dog shampoo nowadays). My wife holds Hazel's collar and gives

CHAPTER 3. WE WISH WE HAD KNOWN

her nice treats while I work on Hazel's rear end. I watched a half-dozen YouTube videos before doing this the first time, and I got better at it over time. (Hint: Be gentle, massage the far side of the gland toward yourself, and do not block the exit route for the fluid—which is on the inner rearward end of the gland, just where you would expect it to be to anoint each poo exiting the butt.) If you do not do it yourself, you may have to pay to take your dog to the vet on a regular, say, three- or four-weekly schedule, which would be yet another cost.

Chapter 4

Unpleasant Surprises

We mentioned a few unpleasant first-dog surprises in the previous chapter. Let us tell you about some more that were memorable.

I was surprised at how fearful Hazel was when I gave her her first swimming lesson. She is, after all, a Gun Dog, bred for working in the water. Nevertheless, when I carried her out into the ocean, in a calm tidal estuary, and gently lowered her into the knee-deep calm seawater, she clung to my leg for dear life, looking for all the world like a fireman sliding down a pole. Her claws scratched up my

CHAPTER 4. UNPLEASANT SURPRISES

legs so badly that my legs were bleeding. After five minutes, however, Hazel was swimming like a fish, and she was eager to get back in for a swim the next day. Her initial dreadful fear surprised me; I have not seen it since in any other circumstance. She is fearful at the Vet, but it is nothing in comparison to her fear during her first swimming lesson.

Another ocean-going surprise/fear is seaweed. Hazel once got caught in some long kelp when swimming in the ocean. Fortunately, she is a strong swimmer with big flipper feet, and she doggy paddled her way over it and broke free in a big splashing effort. At the time, however, I was worried that I was going to have to go into the cold water after her to haul her out.

A man who lives near us had two whippets. He told my wife that he was building a run to keep them separate, so that they did not mate. Three months later, however, I saw him walking the two whippets, and one had a double-row of large dog breasts. He said it had just had puppies. I looked it up, and I was surprised to find that the gestation period in dogs is only about 63 days, plus or minus three, regardless of breeds. So, two months after a moment of inattention with un-fixed dogs, you can get a handful of puppies. Two months later again, there was a flyer in my mailbox, with photos of the two dogs "Blossom" and "Speedy," saying that they had disappeared, and begging for information about them. Our best guess is that he did not have them secured on his property, they ran onto a nearby farm, and the farmer shot them— which they are legally allowed to do if they catch a dog worrying their animals.

A relative boarded his dog at a local kennel (i.e., basically a dog hotel) when he went on vacation. He told me that he was appalled to find that his dog was "skin and bones" when he went to collect him afterwards. Apparently, his dog was not happy and would not eat, and the kennel owners, watching over many dogs, did not (or could not) make enough of an effort to counter that problem.

Similarly, two neighborhood dog owners mentioned to me that their dogs had been injured and contracted "kennel cough," respectively, when they boarded their dogs. So, when we knew that we would be away for a few days, to attend my son's military graduation, we found a local woman who boards dogs, but has space for only one or two. We figured that she could give Hazel the focused attention she needs.

In the months leading up to our trip, we twice

CHAPTER 4. UNPLEASANT SURPRISES

let Hazel stay with the woman for a day-trip, to meet her two dogs and one other dog boarder, and we also tried one additional overnight stay. Each time, we stayed in town, just in case. The dog sitter sent us photos in real time. Hazel had a great time, going to the beach and playing and having dog company. So, when it came time for us to be away for a few days, Hazel got to spend that time in a place she already knew, with a woman she new, and dogs she knew. It all went very well. Of course, it was more expensive than a regular crowded kennel, but you should expect good dog care to be expensive.

When your dog has a problem, it cannot tell you what the problem is. It can, however, communicate via physical behavior. For example, a half-dozen times, Hazel has been walking down the street, and then suddenly stopped and held up her rear leg, the way a human would balance on one leg. The first time, I was surprised and I had no idea what was going on. It turned out that she had stepped on a prickly piece of hedge clipping from a holly hedge. I looked at her paw, and it had a holly leaf stuck in it. So, I pulled the prickly leaf out (directly, so as to not break off the spike). Then I rubbed the paw pad a little and set it down, and off we went. I am now very cautious when walking past a hedge that has been freshly clipped.

The same thing happened (i.e., stopping with a raised paw) when Hazel stepped on a wasp that stung her, just as we were going out of the front gate. At first, I thought it was a prickle, but I saw a wasp squirming around on her paw and I brushed it off. Then Hazel started walking funny, with a wide stance and a hobble. So, I turned around and brought her back inside. She yelped when I touched her paw. The next day, she chewed on it (itchy? painful?) and she chewed off a small patch of fur. It was OK after a couple of days, but even six months later, the fur patch she gnawed off has not fully grown back.

I was walking Hazel in a park and saw what I thought was a Golden Labrador up ahead. It turned out to be a Labrador-Poodle cross. The woman owner said that her dog, Nacho, had rolled in the grass and got an arrow-shaped barbed burrowing grass seed embedded in her fur. A groomer had spotted it after it had caused an abscess. The owner had a vet appointment, and she said that she was fearing a $400 vet bill. She said that grass seeds work their way in, and could get into the bloodstream. A quick internet search reveals that the dog's immune system fights them off as a foreign

CHAPTER 4. UNPLEASANT SURPRISES

body, and there can be infection and an abscess requiring surgical intervention.

The Labrador-Poodle owner said she thought that Hazel's tough Labrador fur coat would fend off the grass seed, whereas her mixed-breed dog's coat would not. I was surprised that the cross between Labrador and Poodle had produced an animal whose fur was so soft that a grass seed could penetrate it. She said she would no longer allow her dog to roll in the grass, but that is easier said than done.

On the subject of rolling in the grass, I was surprised to find that dogs like to roll in the grass where other dogs have peed. Not surprisingly, doing so makes their fur coat stinky.

My wife was walking Hazel on her lead when Hazel suddenly lunged to one side and ate something. It turned out that someone had stepped on a lip balm tube, ejecting a mass of firm white lip balm on the sidewalk, which Hazel ate. She brought the empty tube home to check the contents online. Nothing was toxic, but immediately after lunch Hazel vomited up her stomach contents—which was one of the best possible outcomes.

Another time, someone had left a cup of coffee on a low fence in our neighborhood. I did not notice it, but Hazel sniffed it and took a sip. I heard the slurping sound and I hauled her off immediately, not knowing what it was. I smelled it, and realized that it was coffee, which contains toxic caffeine. Fortunately, the sip was small and Hazel is big, but it could have been much worse with a smaller dog or a less attentive owner.

I was surprised to find that on weekends, at the park or the beach, but rarely in the street, we often meet poorly trained dogs, with owners who look lost and overwhelmed. We have deduced that these are people who work full time and spend very little time with their dog during the week. Often, their dogs are not properly lead trained, so the owners take the dog to the park or the beach, rather than on a neighborhood walk where they must keep the dog on a lead. We think of these dog owners as being a bit like "Sunday drivers," in so far as they only go out on weekends.

I was surprised that the Sunday driver effect is very strong around Christmas and New Year's Day. I guess that an extraordinary number of people who do not usually walk their dog are on holiday at that time, and so there are many people out and about who do not know how to walk their dog in the street, their dogs are also not used to walking with them,

CHAPTER 4. UNPLEASANT SURPRISES

and their dogs are not well socialized. The end result is that around Christmas and New Year's, the park and also the streets and full of unsociable poorly-trained dogs who react badly to me and to Hazel.

A similar effect happens during our school holidays, but it materializes as an unusual number of children out walking dogs, and not necessarily knowing what to do with them.

I was at the beach with my children one weekend, long before we got Hazel. A man was playing with his dog, throwing a ball for it. I was alternately standing still and pacing between the dog and my children, to make sure that the dog did not go near my small children. Each time the man threw the ball, the dog would grab it, and run over to me and drop it at my feet. I would then throw the ball to the confused-looking owner, who would do it again. I suspect now that he was a Sunday driver, and that the dog did not have a strong relationship with him. I suspect that the dog noticed me protecting my children and decided that I was the alpha male to whom the ball should be returned. The moral of the story is that if your dog returns its ball to someone other than you, then you may need to work on your relationship with your dog.

I usually wear gloves when I am walking Hazel because it is often cold where we live. I hold the looped handle of the lead in my left hand and lead itself in my right hand. I am surprised at the speed with which the parts of each glove that touch the lead get worn out. I sewed some patches onto those spots to make them last longer.

I was surprised that as Hazel got older, there were several times a week when she would start whining a little, out of jealousy, we think, when my wife and I have a conversation. She is so socialized and so a part of the family, that when she is left out of a conversation, she sometimes feels ignored and asks for attention. It is not all the time, just sometimes. We noticed the same behavior with our children when they were babies.

If you do not own a dog yet, you might not realize that when you walk your dog past a house where dogs live, there can be an awful barking storm from the house/garden as you approach, are outside of, and then pass by the house where that dog or those dogs live. It can start when you are several houses away, and even if you are on the other side of the road. Your dog generates a response from those dogs that a human passing by without a dog would not generate. So, there are two things to think

CHAPTER 4. UNPLEASANT SURPRISES

about here: Do not be surprised to find that walking your dog generates a lot of noise from neighboring dogs; and, if you are a house owner, with dogs in your house or garden, you may be subjecting your neighbors to a constant barrage of barking when people are walking dogs past your house—and your neighbors will not be happy about it.

One day, a girl (maybe 15 years old) arrived at the park and started playing with her Golden Labrador using a "long lead" that was maybe 30 feet (10 metres) long. Hazel was sitting beside me on a park bench watching every move (she was cooling down after lots of running). After about five minutes of watching, I let Hazel off her lead and she bounced off the bench and trotted over, tail wagging, to say hello. The other dog started bounding towards Hazel, and pulled the owner off her feet and dragged her laying down a few feet across the grass. I mentioned this to my wife when we got home, and she said that was why she stopped using a long lead: The length of a long lead gives a big dog enough leeway to accelerate and build up more than enough momentum to yank you off your feet and/or damage your wrist, elbow, shoulder or lower back.

I am surprised that Hazel, with her super-sensitive nose, uses it as a battering ram. She walks down our hallway and bangs her sensitive nose right against the dining room door to open it. She does the same at my office, when she goes to see a favorite colleague. Sometimes, however, the door is shut, and it makes a terrible "thump!" sound when she rams into it. She is, however, getting a bit better at judging whether a door is ajar or closed.

Hazel is on a pooping-clock. She needs to poop around 10:30AM and around 4:30PM. So, we schedule walks for 10AM and 4PM. Unfortunately, Mother Nature is not on a sympathetic clock. So, that means that we are sometimes out walking Hazel in awful weather (pouring rain, freezing cold, strong winds, etc.) Hazel is a Labrador, so she has a semi-waterproof coat and she likes the cold. This means that Hazel may be having a good time, while my fingertips are going numb.

One day, the weather forecast was that we would get one month's worth of rain in three days—and it had already started. I put on my boots and woolens and waterproofs and put Hazel's raincoat on and we walked to the park to throw a ball in the heavy rain. We were out for about 75 minutes, walking, playing, and walking back. She had a great time. When we got home, I mentioned to my wife that I saw no

CHAPTER 4. UNPLEASANT SURPRISES

other dogs out and about (there are usually lots at that time). She said "Are you surprised?" Yes, actually, I was. Dogs need to get out and get some exercise. I guess, however, that on awful-weather days many dog owners chose to stay inside with a dog—who may be getting "cabin fever" from being stuck inside. Ask yourself whether you are the sort of person who does not want to go out walking in the pouring rain, or when it is freezing cold with a gale blowing. If so, then either you will need to go out anyway, and you will not like it, or you will not go out, and your dog will likely get cabin fever.

When walking Hazel, we met another Chocolate Labrador at the park. I did not notice, at first, that he was missing his right eye. His owner told me that "Bruno" was nine years old, and two and a half years earlier he had been running in the bush and had run right into a low poking branch that wrecked his eye. The owner said that Bruno was a happy dog getting on with enjoying his life, but that sometimes he bumped into things, like car trailer hitches, because he could not see on one side. My daughter joked that they should rename Bruno to Uno. We fear the same thing happening to Hazel, who happily charges through undergrowth in the bush with reckless abandon.

When my wife was walking Hazel on a track near the ocean, Hazel once stopped dead in her tracks and refused to go on. It took my wife a minute to figure out the problem. A large sea lion was snoozing, camouflaged, on the rocks beside the path just ahead. An adult male New Zealand sea lion can weigh as much as 1,000 pounds (450kg). Hazel did the same thing with me at the same spot another time, and there was a dead seal on those same rocks. After Hazel stopped, I stared and stared, looking for the cause, expecting to find a dead cormorant/shag or a dead fish, but our seals are so well camouflaged that even though I was expecting to find something it took me more than a minute to spot it.

Hazel has bare feet all the time. So, I have to look out for her. Several times, I have had to stop, and pick up Hazel and carry her 10 or 20 paces because of broken glass in the street. For example, on one occasion, we were downtown and attempting to cross at a busy intersection when we faced so much glass that we could not go around it. Drunken hooligans break bottles, especially near the University. So, I am especially cautious there. Hazel weighs about 55–60 pounds (25kg–27kg), so carrying her far can be a bit of a strain.

We always restrain Hazel in the car. She sits

CHAPTER 4. UNPLEASANT SURPRISES

in the back seat and has a belt that clips onto her harness and into a seatbelt socket. We have the window open a crack so that she can snoot out the window, smelling where she is going. We keep the car doors locked. I assumed everyone did that, but a guy I see at the park all the time with two dogs, turned up one day with only one dog. I asked where his other dog was, and he said it had jumped out of the open window of the car while he was driving down the road, and got killed by the car behind him. He said that he thought maybe his dog saw another dog and wanted to say hello.

I was surprised that parents with very small children, even ones too small to be walking yet, will come up to me and shove their child's face right into Hazel's face, without ever having even met me or Hazel before. Every dog is different, and doing this widely is surely a recipe for disaster. For example, a dad carrying a small girl did this a block from our house when Hazel was about six months old and still very jumpy. The little girl was terrified. When Hazel starting prancing around in excitement, the dad backed off, looking very surprised. I am very cautious when Hazel is near any child, because any animal is unpredictable and any child is unpredictable, but now I am also cautious because of unpredictable adults.

Ninety-nine times out of 100, I pick up Hazel's poo. The only times I do not are when Hazel perches on a precipice (e.g., a sea cliff), and is balancing there to do her poo, and I would risk death collecting it, or if she runs off into the bush and I cannot see her and I can only guess she did a poo. Sometimes, however, I simply cannot find her poo, even after serious searching.

For example, in fall/autumn, I was surprised at how difficult it can be to spot a fresh poo in the grass, among the fallen leaves. It is especially difficult in the half-light at dusk. If Hazel runs away from me in the park and squats 50 yards (50 metres) away, and then I have to find it, it can be quite a time consuming search. Once, when walking on lead, she stepped off the sidewalk and pooped in someone's front yard. Even though I watched her do it, on her lead, only a few feet from me, I simply could not find it after several minutes of solid searching among the leaves; I had to leave without finding it.

I am surprised at the number of dog walkers who do not pick up their dog's poo. I often see dog owners walking well ahead of their dog, and purposely not looking back. Not picking up a poo gives all

CHAPTER 4. UNPLEASANT SURPRISES

dog owners a bad name, even though only a very few are guilty. So, when I am walking Hazel, and I pick up her poo using a poo bag, I often choose not to tie the bag up until I get to the nearest garbage can. Then, I will often carefully use that same bag to pick up one or two other dog poos on the way to the garbage can. It is disgusting, but it helps clean up the street and reduce bad opinions of other dog owners.

I am surprised that Hazel has pooed on her tennis ball by mistake a few times. She runs off to chase her ball at the park, retrieves it, then decides she needs to poo. She drops the ball and gets into position, which may involve inching forward a bit, and then she accidentally poos on it.

I was surprised at how many other dog owners hit their dogs. Invariably, those dogs are badly behaved. In my opinion, hitting your dog is a foolish thing to do. It does not improve their behavior. Instead, they fear being hit and have no idea what to do to please you. They can fail to respond to commands because they fear being hit for doing something wrong. In contrast, our practice of denying affection for bad behavior and giving rewards for good behavior seems to work amazingly well.

Dogs pick up on cues. So, Hazel sees me getting

her little box of kibble ready to reward her as we walk, and she gets off her chair and sits on the floor, ready to get harnessed up. At the same time, she does not like rainy days. So, if she sees me getting her raincoat ready, she gets stubborn and can refuse to get off of her comfortable chair.

On a half-dozen occasions, Hazel has stuck her nose right into some visitor's crotch. Most of the time it is someone that Hazel knows well, and that person is female. Sometimes it is some old guy wearing old dirty clothes. It is slightly embarrassing but they usually just push her away; maybe they are used to it.

We have other pets. Hazel wants to hurt some of them sometimes. This is distressing to the pets and the children. Hazel has gotten her nose scratched by our cat and by the neighbor's cat several times. I do not think Hazel means them any harm, but she wants to play with them or chase them for fun. Of course, playing with a cat might leave it dead. So, I do not blame them for scratching Hazel's nose.

Hazel has been attacked multiple times by other (usually poorly socialized) dogs. The other dogs typically latch their jaws onto the back of Hazel's neck. I was worried one time that I was going to have to kill another dog and then deal with the an-

CHAPTER 4. UNPLEASANT SURPRISES

gry owner. Fortunately, immediately yanking Hazel backwards via her lead and simultaneously booting the other dog like a rugby ball was enough. Hazel screamed like a small child when she was attacked on that occasion, which was distressing. I see the owner several times a week, and I give him a wave, but we keep our dogs apart; such is life.

I am now of the opinion that if you walk a dog in public, you have to accept that sometimes another dog will attack your dog. If your dog is injured, has a large vet bill, or is killed, then I think you have no cause for complaint and should not expect the other dog owner to compensate you in any way; violent dog encounters are just part of the fabric of life with a dog. If you cannot accept that, then do not bring a dog into your life.

Something else to consider is that your dog may attack another dog or a child. In New Zealand, the law says that if I let a friend walk my dog, and my dog attacks a dog or a child, it is my friend, not I, who may get prosecuted. Given the very high percentage of non-owners I see out walking dogs, this is worth remembering.

One day, my wife took Hazel to the park and let her off lead just where the car park meets the grass. Another woman was standing unseen between two nearby parked cars and her two small dogs ran over and started barking at Hazel. Hazel let out a few enormous woofs, to scare the aggressive little dogs away, and then Hazel turned her back on the little aggressive dogs and walked to the grass to play. The woman owner, however, started yelling at my wife, telling her that Hazel was a bad dog and that Hazel and my wife should be reported to the City Council. My wife was politely apologetic, but only because the woman was obviously nuts. (Why else did she react that way when her dogs started the fight and all Hazel did was bark and walk away without even making any contact?) The woman proceeded to shout at my wife as she took Hazel to the park. When my wife was 100 yards (100 metres) away, the woman was still shouting and was pointing my wife and Hazel out to another person who had just arrived in the parking lot. I guess the moral of the story is that there are crazy people everywhere, and even if another person's dogs start a fight, you might still get yelled at by the owner.

One day, Hazel was walking off-lead in a nearby valley, when she found a big wild apple tree with hundreds of big red apples on it. There were also hundreds of apples on the ground. She gorged herself on them before I could get down the steep bank

CHAPTER 4. UNPLEASANT SURPRISES

and haul her off of them. Her poo was very soft the next day, but otherwise there were no other side effects.

I am surprised at the mess that Hazel makes in the car. We put down a blanket for her, but she still manages to mess up the seat back, the foot well, the little rim (above the rocker panel) that you step over to get into the car, and the door window sill where she rests her chin. It is a mixture of mud/dirt from the park, dog hair and dog slobber. We upgraded our vehicle recently. For our newer car, my wife got a full rear seat cover, and I cut some carpet to go where Hazel's feet step as she is getting in. The seat cover was, however, too slippery for Hazel's paw pads. So, my wife sewed some hook/loop tape to the cover and we stuck a soft blanket on top. It was several hours of effort on our parts to achieve the final product.

We get occasional dog-related injuries. For example, my wife got knocked over in the dog park by a pack of dogs running with Hazel. My wife hit her head and had to go to the doctor. When dogs run together, they often look over their shoulder at the other dogs they are running with, rather than looking at where they are going. (From experience, I think it is best to bend your knees and lower your center of gravity when a pack of dogs is charging at you; I see other people doing the same. It reduces injuries if you get hit.) Twice, Hazel has pulled me over while we were walking down a steep hill, where the surface was wet grass with some mud; on one of those occasions I hit the back of my head, possibly on a tree root, and I may have been briefly unconscious. I was groggy for 24 hours afterwards. Another time, Hazel pulled my wife off her feet in the street, causing minor bruising. I have gotten small cuts and scratches on my fingers from her teeth, and bleeding scratches on my bare legs from her claws. I have gotten shoulder and lower back injuries from Hazel yanking on her lead when suddenly lunging for something, etc. These are many more injuries than we were expecting. A smaller dog would perhaps have caused fewer injuries because it would not have been able to pull us off our feet.

One of the surprises that contributes to these injuries is Hazel's sheer strength. Although she is small for a Labrador, her thigh muscles are six inches (15cm) wide, which is about the same as mine, she has two strong front legs, and she has a very low center of gravity. So, when she lunges for something, she can rip tissue in your shoulders

CHAPTER 4. UNPLEASANT SURPRISES

or lower back, causing painful long-lasting injuries; a male Labrador would be even stronger. The two-point harness and hand grips discussed in the next chapter goes a long way toward having greater control of her strength, and we are planning to do some lunging-avoidance training, but this is likely to be an issue until she gets much older.

I was washing dishes and accidentally knocked two pieces or crockery together and chipped a bowl. The sharp chip was 3/4 of an inch (2cm) long. It shot sideways onto the floor. Hazel gulped it up in a fraction of a second, before I could stop her. This could be rally bad for some breeds. Fortunately, Labradors have a cast iron gut.

We have to be careful not to leave anything within reach of Hazel in the kitchen. Hazel has grabbed a wooden mixing spoon, the handle of a spatula, food being prepared on a counter, etc. She tries to reach and lick anything she can get to, like mixing bowls, plates of food being prepared, etc. She goes up on her hind legs and turns her head sideways and pushes her tongue out as far as it can go. Every time we open the dishwasher to put things in it she tries to stick her head in it. It is like having a mischievous furry gremlin/imp in the house who is always watching and always waiting to pounce on any opportunity that presents itself.

I was walking Hazel through the downtown area and she stopped and started sniffing like crazy at a store frontage, and on the sidewalk in front of that store. Hazel was very distracted and focused. The storekeeper came out to say hello, and I pointed out Hazel's odd behavior. The storekeeper said that there had been an assault the previous evening, and that the front of her store and sidewalk was splattered with blood. She had cleaned it up first thing, but Hazel's nose was not fooled. I pointed out to the storekeeper some blood stains on the front of the store that Hazel had noticed and that the storekeeper had missed.

Finally, for this chapter, this is a gut-wrenchingly disgusting story. It makes me feel sick to even write it down. Stop reading here and skip to the next chapter if you are sensitive to awful/disgusting images that you cannot get out of your head. When walking Hazel at a local park, I met a young couple who said that on the previous day they had taken their dog to a different park in town, and that several homeless people were living there. A homeless person had pooed in the bushes at the edge of the park (identifiable by toilet paper, I think) and their dog ate the human poo before the

CHAPTER 4. UNPLEASANT SURPRISES

owners could stop it. When they got home their dog vomited the partially digested human poo up onto their living room carpet, which the owners then had to clean up. Happy times!

Chapter 5

Other Surprises

Unlike the unpleasant first-dog surprises in the previous chapter, some surprises are harmless, and some are even entertaining. We walk through some of these lighter cases in this chapter.

I was surprised at how quickly Hazel grew over the first few months. Her rate of growth reminded me of those science fiction movies where a cute little space creature doubles in size every few days until to takes over the space craft. (No, her growth rate was not quite that rapid.) If I had known about Hazel's incredible growth rate in advance, I would have taken more photos and videos when Hazel was a cute little roly-poly puppy. By the time Hazel was

CHAPTER 5. OTHER SURPRISES

one year old, she was fully grown.

I am surprised to find that we talk about Hazel's poo almost every day. Did she do one this morning? Was it healthy? If not, what was wrong, etc.? The same thing happens when you have a baby and the frequency and health of the child's poo tells you about the health of the baby. Just like a baby, a dog cannot talk to you and tell you how it feels. So, looking at its poo tells you a lot that it cannot say. I make no apologies for the extraordinary number of dog poo stories in this book; it is a daily part of dog ownership.

It seems silly now, but I was surprised that fresh dog poo is hot the first time I picked it up (through the bag obviously; I am never touching it with my bare hands if I can help it because of the bacteria, viruses, parasites and other harmful pathogens). On a cold winter morning, Hazel's poos give off steam on the ground (which can make them easier to spot amongst fallen leaves).

Similarly, in my ignorance, I was surprised to learn that it is typically only the male dogs who pee against lampposts, walls, etc. I never really noticed before owning a dog that the female dogs do not do that. Instead, 95% of the time, they squat and pee on the ground. The other 5% of the time, they will lean a little toward some lamppost or similar, and try to pee on it.

I had heard, many years ago, that a dog's mouth is very clean. Well, I beg to differ. If Hazel has just been licking her bum, then her mouth smells like dog bum. I see neighbors, friends and strangers who encourage Hazel to lick their face, and they are perfectly happy when she does so, but I never let her put her mouth on my face if I can help it—I know where it has been.

I was surprised that on popular long walking tracks, dog walkers often leave their doggy poo bags beside the track, intending to pick them up on the return journey. That is because poo is such an unpleasant thing to carry. I choose, instead, to put a loose loop in the top of the bag and clip it to the handle of the lead. Then, I have only one thing in that hand (i.e., the lead handle), and it is far enough from my nose that the smell is reduced 98%.

One day, my wife drove our car downtown to go shopping several miles away, while I walked away from our house for a walk in our own neighborhood. After an hour of walking around a big circuit, 15-month old Hazel and I came to the busy little shopping center not far from our house, and Hazel suddenly went nuts. She was walking north, then east,

CHAPTER 5. OTHER SURPRISES

then south, then west, whining and pining, nose-to-the-ground, searching for something within a 10-foot (three-metre) radius. She ignored the many people walking by. I could not figure out what she was looking for. I thought someone must have dropped some food, like a meat pie or a sausage, but there was nothing there.

After two full minutes of fruitless searching, I gave up and hauled Hazel reluctantly off towards the parking lot we usually walk through on the way home. There, just beyond our original line of sight, the second car we came to was ours, with my wife sitting in it. I was surprised, at least initially, that Hazel must have picked up my wife's scent, as distinguished from those of all the other people shopping, and known that my wife had walked through there a few minutes earlier. I have never seen her search so frantically for something or whine so much. It was an interesting unplanned blind experiment in scent trailing.

Hazel was tied to a post outside the drug store while I popped in for a few minutes. I was watching her through the windows while I was waiting in line. She was sitting and watching people come and go. She was wagging her tail (sweeping the sidewalk) when anyone made eye contact. A young woman came over to Hazel, crouched down, and patted her as I watched. Hazel was very tail-waggy and happy. The woman was still there when I came out. She said her dog had died and she missed him. We talked for a few minutes. I am surprised by how many people tell me about their dead dog(s) while patting Hazel. I think these episodes are cathartic for the people who lost their dogs. The frequency with which this happens reflects the large number of dogs in the community, the short lifespan of a dog, and the impact a dog has on family life. Dogs drain your resources when they arrive, and they leave a vacuum when they depart.

One young woman was almost in tears when she patted Hazel outside my office building, telling me that they had to put their Chocolate Labrador down two months earlier. I asked how old her dog had been, and she said "14 years." I said, sympathetically, that was a good life for a Chocolate Labrador. (They tend to live a couple of years fewer than Golden or Black Labradors). She seemed kind of annoyed, however, saying that several people had told her that, but that it was no comfort. I now wish I had said something different. She looked about 20; I should have asked her dog's name, acknowledged that she must have had her dog since she was a lit-

CHAPTER 5. OTHER SURPRISES

tle girl, and that its loss must have been awful for her; I will do that next time.

We bought a new fabric-covered arm chair. One day, my wife shooed the cat away when it tried to scratch it. Hazel saw this and then jumped in to start chasing the cat. Now, each time the cat tries to scratch that chair or the carpet, Hazel jumps up and chases her away. We are slightly worried for the cat, but we think it is more likely that Hazel will get hurt. Unlike almost every other form of purposeful training, this accidental training did not involve food or praise. Hazel appears to be doing it just to please us.

Hazel and I got caught at the park in a sudden heavy downpour of rain in the winter. Neither of us had brought our rain jackets with us. So, we huddled together under a big tree until the rain passed. I was surprised at how much heat she gave off. Now, when she sits beside me on a park bench, I slide over right beside her and she gives off enough heat in the winter to keep me warm while she is resting.

We had had Hazel for a few weeks, and I was giving her a belly rub. I played with her big flipper feet, and was amazed to find that they are webbed. I had never in my life heard of a dog with webbed feet; they make her an amazing swimmer. I mention her webbed feet to other people sometimes, for example when a small child is patting her, because I think they will find it interesting. The parent(s) usually laugh, because they think I am joking. Some children find it interesting; others find it kind of awful—like finding that your schoolyard friend has webbed feet.

I was surprised to find that when Hazel sits on the polished wood floor in our kitchen, her back feet slowly slide out sideways, and she then readjusts her stance. Then it happens again, and again, etc. Her leather paw pads give her no grip on such surfaces. So, I usually walk her off the wooden floor if I want her to sit. As a consequence, when she hangs out in the kitchen, she tends to flop down on her side, rather than sitting, as she does elsewhere, to avoid her feet sliding. She is even a little reluctant to obey a "sit" command if she is in the kitchen, because she does not like her feet sliding out (it took me a while to figure out the reason for her reluctance). When she sits beside me on a park bench, I usually put my arm around her and drop my hand down to hold her back foot, to stop it sliding away out from under her on the wooden bench.

Although Hazel is a dark Chocolate Labrador, I was surprised that her mother (whom we met)

CHAPTER 5. OTHER SURPRISES

is a Golden Labrador and her father is a Black Labrador. I did not know that genetics could work that way with coat color for dogs. Her mother was from New Zealand but her father was based in California; it was a male-order romance.

Hazel's very dark coat means that she disappears into the background when she is running in the bush or even just walking in the street in the evening. I often put a high-vis reflector belt around her waist, looped through her harness. Sometimes, it is all I can see of her in the late evening. It makes us both show up much better in low-light situations, and it makes Hazel show up in situations where drivers or pedestrians are not necessarily expecting to see a dog.

I have been very surprised by peoples' reactions to her when she is wearing her reflector belt. Some people who want to pat her assume that she is a service dog, and so they ask if it is OK to pat her (like you would ask a guide dog's owner). Other folks assume that she is some sort of support dog, and therefore assume that she is very well trained and friendly (which she is); this positive first impression of her serves as an icebreaker, because people are more attracted to her when they think that she must be well trained. Hazel loves the attention.

I was surprised that most people just assume that Hazel is a male. Nine times out of ten, people ask "What's his name?" or "How old is he?" I watched a Netflix dog training documentary, about a dog trainer in California. He said that most people are scared of dark-colored dogs, and think of them as aggressive. He said that such perceptions of aggression make it difficult to find homes for dark-colored dogs if they are in a dog shelter/pound. I think people assume that my dark-colored dog may be aggressive and associate aggression with maleness and therefore assume that Hazel is a male. It is odd, because male Labradors are typically much larger than Hazel and male Labradors often have a different facial structure to female Labradors.

I was at first surprised that some people jump and dance around in terror if they walk around a corner and come face to face with Hazel. This includes people at my office who have met her a dozen times already when she was on her absolute best behavior. I think "cynophobia" (i.e., fear of dogs, pronounced *sigh-no-foh-bee-a*) is a deeply-held fear, especially among women; it may be further accentuated by her dark coat.

Sometimes, I ask people before getting into an elevator whether it is OK to bring Hazel in; they

CHAPTER 5. OTHER SURPRISES

have always said yes. Once, however, when I was about to get into an elevator in my office building with Hazel, I did not ask the sole male occupant and he stepped back and said "I am a little afraid of dogs" in a meek voice, (in fact, he looked terrified); I said "thanks for telling me; I will get the next one."

It took about a year to train Hazel to not jump up on people when she is excited. We did it by asking people to turn their back on Hazel if she jumps up (i.e., denying affection). We combined this with positive reinforcement (e.g., kind words, physical affection, and treats) if she stays seated to get attention; it has worked wonderfully. I was very pleasantly surprised at how effective Hazel's training became once we denied affection, attention or treats for her bad behavior and rewarded her good behavior. Those two actions, when combined, have been the key to her training. One consequence is that Hazel now looks to me for a reward after almost every encounter where she sits to get attention from strangers, or when she is quiet when a small dog barks at her.

Let me give another example of this training approach. As a tiny roly-poly puppy, Hazel did not yet know how to behave. She had spiky little teeth that easily unintentionally drew blood when she played with us. So, to train her out of these biting accidents, every time she bit us (usually on a hand), even playfully, we denied affection, and every time she licked us (usually on a hand), we said "good licky-lick" in a positive voice, and gave her cuddles and a treat. After a few short months, Hazel stopped biting, and has not properly bitten anyone since then. Sometimes, however, when she is excited, she will accidentally nip my finger when I give her a treat on a walk. I say "Ouch!" very loudly, with a sudden intake of breath, so that she knows that she hurt me. Then I find an excuse to give her another treat, and she is always very gentle that next time.

We allow one exception to our no-jumping-up rule, which we call a "Hazel hug." We noticed that when any two of our family members had a hug in Hazel's presence, always indoors, Hazel always bounds over and tries to join in. It seems innocent enough, so, we have allowed it. We sometimes, however, exploit a Hazel hug to get her off the couch at bed time, or something similar: We have a hug, and she gets up off the couch and comes over to join in. Then, it is off to bed (or off to wherever we need her to go). It is a gentle way of getting her to move

CHAPTER 5. OTHER SURPRISES

when she does not want to.

Only once in four years has Hazel tried to replicate her "Hazel hug" behavior in public. I was out walking her, and I stopped to talk to a woman neighbor that Hazel and I have both known for several years. Then a friend of my neighbor walked up and they talked for a few minutes, and then the two women had a goodbye hug, and Hazel surprised me by trying to join in. I pulled her away, and explained to them why she did it. I think it happened that one time only because Hazel has known that woman for several years, and maybe views her as part of her extended family.

We are surprised by how long Hazel holds her pee. She wakes up at maybe 5AM and walks about a bit in the house, but we tell her to go back to sleep, and she does so for an hour. Then we take her outside for a pee at 6AM.

I was surprised at the noises Hazel makes and her physical behavior when she sees someone she wants a stroke from. She makes high-pitched whining pining *hmmm* sounds, almost like a human vocalizing but with its mouth closed, and she walk/runs to them almost like she is hopping over things; almost like a child's rocking horse rocking back and forth. Then she sits at their feet, sidles over to them, leans against their legs, and looks up at them waiting for a stroke. She loves people who are excited to see her and who give her vigorous strokes, scratching her back and sides and tummy, etc.

We were surprised that when we took Hazel to a park on a very cold frosty morning, she started doing "zoomies" on the crunchy frosty grass. A zoomie is also known as a Frenetic Random Activity Period (FRAP). It is when a dog has a sudden, intense burst of bounding energy. It runs around like a crazy animal, often back and forth in a straight line, or in circles or ovals. The dog will contract its rear legs further forward than usual when running, the way a Greyhound does when sprinting. It does not last long. It is a sign of excited happiness, and is most common in young dogs. Sometimes Hazel will do zoomies in the house, especially if she came back from a walk, but did not get a good run (maybe because the park was too wet).

Similarly, on some days, we walk to the park in light rain and cold temperatures, and there are no dogs to play with and the grass is too wet and/or muddy to play ball. So, as soon as we get home, Hazel grabs a toy and we play chase from room to room and up and down the hallway. Keep this in

CHAPTER 5. OTHER SURPRISES

mind, because if your house does not have a long hallway with big rooms at each end, then your dog may not be able to run freely in the house, and your dog may get cabin fever on cold/wet days.

To the contrary, sometimes after a vigorous park visit, Hazel gets home and she immediately grabs a toy and start bounding around the house wanting to play chase. I thought she had had enough exercise, but she wants to play more!

We have a bowl of water for Hazel on the polished wood floor in the kitchen. I was surprised that we had to put it on a rubber mat. The mat has a rim around the edge to contain spills. Otherwise, Hazel slops water all over the floor. Also, I was surprised that we have to empty the bowl, rinse it out and refill it several times a day. That cleaning out is partly because we throw food in the water for her at meal times, and the food and her saliva make the water stinky if it is not changed several times a day.

Hazel is a Gun Dog, bred to retrieve things (e.g., ducks shot out of the sky above a lake, or fishing nets in the water). She is an amazing swimmer. She loves playing in the water at the beach or at a nearby calm estuary. I was surprised, however, that she does not like walks on rainy days. She will even refuse to obey a sit command on a rainy day. She also avoids walking through rain puddles on the sidewalk. I think she dislikes rainy walks because the rain interferes with her sense of smell, and she fails to obey a sit command on a rainy day because it is cold here, and she would get her bum cold and wet. I do not know why she avoids puddles; maybe she cannot tell how deep they are from her low angle, or with her poor visual depth perception or poor visual acuity (discussed later). Maybe she does not like the *feel* of puddles on her paw pads— she also does not like walking on coarse gravel.

On a related note, we take Hazel swimming at a local estuary. The water is often relatively calm and only knee deep close to shore. We throw a stick and she bounds in, but I was surprised the first time we did this that for the first few steps into the water she tries not to get too wet, bounding up and down trying to keep her tummy dry. Only when she realizes that she *has* to swim does she go all out and just happily dive in.

Hazel's head is low to the ground. On a windy day at the beach, she can get sand in her eyes that would only be buffeting our legs. So, we typically avoid the beach on very windy days. We do, however, have goggles for her (called "doggles"), that we

CHAPTER 5. OTHER SURPRISES

have used at the beach on windy days. They look like a skier's reflective goggles. We have also used them on very sunny days at home when she goes and lies on a light-colored deck in the sun. Unlike her muzzle (discussed later), Hazel has no problem with wearing her doggles.

I was surprised that on Guy Fawkes Day (November 5, when people let off fireworks in their gardens and in the local parks), Hazel had no fear of the fireworks and was happy to snooze through them on the sofa. Our cat, however, was hiding under the bed in the spare room. We think her Gun Dog breeding is part of Hazel's lack of fear of loud sudden noises.

I am sometimes woken in the early morning, or during an afternoon nap, by loud barking, or a wet nose on my cheek, or a lick of my hand. That surprised me at first. It reminds me of our first night at home after our first child was born: I awoke in the small hours, exhausted and fuzzy headed, wondering why on Earth there was a baby crying loudly, as if it were actually in my house.

I was surprised the first time I saw Hazel chewing her back claws, while curled up on the sofa. I thought maybe they were long and needed clipping, but they were not. She just gives them a little chew every now and then. I had assumed before we got her that I would have to clip her claws, but she walks in the city streets so much that the sidewalk wears them down, and we have never had to clip them. Perhaps we will have to do so when she is older.

I was surprised by Hazel's context-specific growling. She growls if she sees one of her archenemy dogs in the street; and, if I intervene quickly enough, I can stop her barking. Hazel growls if she is confused (e.g., a woman walking towards us with a wheelbarrow confused her, as did a man in a kaftan walking towards us using a Zimmer frame). She growls if you touch her back feet too much, and that is a warning to stop. Hazel growls if you tickle her tummy, but she really likes it, and that is a contented growl. She also growls if she is sitting beside you on the sofa and you *do not* tickle her tummy, when she wants you to. The growls sound mostly very similar but have different meanings; you have to interpret them based upon the context.

I am surprised that even though Hazel has been in our car several times a week for over four years, she does not recognize our car. When I have Hazel at work, my wife meets me at the office, and parks on the street outside the main doors of my office

CHAPTER 5. OTHER SURPRISES

building. Hazel and I exit the building, but Hazel pulls me over to the edge of the sidewalk, and shuffles sideways, getting ready to enter whatever car is parked right outside, even though half the time it is not our car that is right there. Hazel even tried to get into a full-sized fire engine that was parked there for a false alarm in a nearby building, not noticing that it was a giant red fire engine and not our four-door sedan. (Dogs see red as grey, so I guess the color did not stand out, but it was so much bigger than our car!) It makes me think that Hazel would happily jump into any car, bus, truck, fire engine, etc. that pulls up, and could easily be dog-napped if she were on the loose.

I was sitting beside Hazel in the back seat of our car as we were driving around town. She was belted in. I was surprised to see that she leans into the corners, to keep her balance. I could also see that she was tightening her claws (like us digging in our finger nails) as we went around corners.

I was walking 15-month old Hazel on her lead through the University campus, when she spotted some ducks in the river. She almost yanked my arm off its hinges. So, I set her free, and the end result looked like a *Tom and Jerry* cartoon. She bounded into the river at top speed, and chased the ducks upstream in repeated bursts, as they took off and landed again several times. It looked like a clumsy hippo chasing a gazelle through a river. When she was reasonably far away, my wife gave two toots on her dog whistle, and Hazel came bounding back at double speed, water flying everywhere. It was very comical. I see now why *Tom and Jerry* cartoons were so popular.

Other dogs like to lick Hazel's ears. I was surprised by this and by how stinky she gets if we do not wash her almost immediately afterwards, because dog saliva gets very stinky when it dries.

You may be surprised at how dirty your dog gets when playing at the park. Hazel is such a dark chocolate color that the dirt does not show on her so much, but on other light-colored dogs we can see that it looks awful. It is not just the wet grass, or mud, or other debris. When dogs run and play with each other, they tend to slobber on each other. That white foam slobber may disappear quickly, but, like having their ears licked, it gets very stinky very quickly. So, your dog may need a wash after playing at the park, even on a dry warm summer day.

You and your dog may be disappointed when that happy looking Border Collie playing at the

CHAPTER 5. OTHER SURPRISES

park runs right past you and your dog with zero interest in socializing. Sometimes, this leads to "parallel play," where your dog runs around with the other dog, but might as well be invisible as far as the other dog is concerned. (We heard the term "parallel play" used quite often when our children were in kindergarten and primary school; boy children are more likely to engage in parallel play than girl children, who are more likely to engage with their peers.) Hazel has, however, over the course of several years, made friends with one local Border Collie, who always stops what she is doing at the park and comes over to get a pat from me and to say hello to Hazel; that is very unusual for that breed.

I was surprised to find, when checking Hazel's mouth at around three-and-a-half years of age, that she had a chipped rear molar. One of the peaks of one molar was gone. She must have chewed on something very solid, maybe a stick or bone or an accidental rock. It looked otherwise fine and has not caused any problems. I often say to my wife, "Well, that might happen naturally in the wild if she were a wolf;" it is not of much comfort.

I was surprised that by age four years, Hazel did not have as much energy as she used to. She was getting tired on walks and could not jog as far at the park without getting puffed. A four-year old medium-large dog is like a 30-year old human. So, perhaps a little bit of a slowdown is roughly what you might expect at that age.

Hazel lifts her head and closes her eyes in bliss when you tickle her under the chin. Strangers often remark upon it. I was surprised that an animal would close its eyes with a stranger. However, I did a test where I covered Hazel's eyes and held a treat two inches from her nose. She immediately snapped it up. She knew what it was, which direction it was, and how far it was. I think her super-nose (we call it her "super-snooter") gives her so much information that her eyes are not as important as I had previously thought. This super power could be useful in old age, if her vision begins to fail.

I am surprised at the number of people who see us in the street and ask, "Are you training him?" Some of them do not understand that, like most dog owners, we train Hazel in basic skills every single day, starting from when we get up in the morning. Some people see us training in the street, and ask if we are training her for some sort of dog show, but that might also be because she looks like a pure-bred animal.

CHAPTER 5. OTHER SURPRISES

I am surprised by how many people ask if we take Hazel hunting (they mean ducks or pigs/boars, I think) or if she is a working farm dog. We tell them that although she is bred as a Gun Dog, she is just a family pet and we have never taken her hunting and she has never worked on a farm.

At the university, a foreign student stopped me as I was leaving my office building because she wanted to pat Hazel, filming the episode on her smart phone. She asked me "what does he do?" (again, assuming Hazel is a male). I thought she meant does she do any tricks (which is something that children often ask me), but I asked her to clarify. She meant "what is her job?" That is, is she a guide dog, is she a guard dog, is she a drug-sniffing dog, etc. Someone outside the Police Station also asked me if she is a drug-sniffing dog. I said no, but that she could be a meat-pie-sniffing dog, because she tried to grab my neighbor's meat pie from his hand when he was patting her; he thought that was funny.

My neighbors' two small boys are always very excited to see Hazel. They are about four and six years old, respectively. So, Hazel is older than one boy and younger than the other one. I am surprised by how many questions they ask: Can we feed her, can we see her teeth, why does she have such big teeth, can we shake her paw, can we see her paw pads, does she poo, does she poo beside your house, how does she know to shake my hand when I put my hand out? (Those questions were all in the space of about 60 seconds.) I am surprised by the boys' excitement. I hold Hazel tightly (sometimes holding her head) when she meets them, because she is taller than the smaller boy and could knock him over.

I give Hazel a bath about once a week; more often if she runs in the mud, less often if she does not need it. I usually wash her outside on a brick patio behind the house. I fill two or three buckets with warm water. She sees me getting ready and then goes to the back door and waits to be let out. Then she goes and stands in the spot. Then I clip her lead to her collar and hook the other end onto a tree stump. I was surprised that although she is keen to get out, keen to go to the spot, and knows what is coming, she still squirms to get away from me when I start dumping cups full of warm water on her and rubbing her down. She knows it is her duty to stand there, but she still squirms.

I was also surprised that, like a child, Hazel seems to sleep better at night after a warm

CHAPTER 5. OTHER SURPRISES

bath/shower.

We have several dog brushes for brushing Hazel's fur. After about a year, I stopped using any of them. Hazel does not like them, they irritate her skin, and they do not work very well. Instead, I just use a human comb. I was surprised, however, that the length of the teeth on the comb makes a difference: The longer the teeth, the better. Also, the comb tends to work best when Hazel is damp, after a shower. That is, it is easier to remove loose fur that is damp, and it is easier to make her fur tidy when it is damp, than when she is dry.

Another Chocolate Labrador owner stopped me in the park and asked me about his Labrador's dandruff. He could not get it to stop. I told him that I had found that even the gentlest dog shampoo irritated Hazel's skin and caused dandruff, and that the dog brushes seemed to do the same. I told him that I almost never use any soaps or shampoos on Hazel, and that I use a comb, not a brush, and that her coat is very healthy as a result.

I was surprised to find that almost every dog is "public property," at least to some extent. Many people come up and pat Hazel. Ninety percent of them ask first, verbally or via body language, if it is OK to pat her. I do the same to other dogs and dog owners, but only the nice or interesting ones. I do not think many people are going up to pat the dogs that look ugly or dangerous. Keep that in mind when you pick a breed.

Hazel has her own social life, her own favorite dog friends, her own favorite human friends, and her own arch-enemy neighborhood dogs. In that sense, she is her own independent little "person." Other people have relationships with her and come up to talk to her and pat her, and Hazel goes up to other people, or picks people out and plants her feet and wags her tail to get them to come to her. So, on some level, you never really "own" a dog the way that you own a car. For example, strangers are not getting into your car in the street every day, but people will stop to talk to and pat your dog every day, sometimes without asking.

I was surprised at how attached Hazel is to people outside our nuclear family that she has known since she was a little puppy; the same is true of dogs she has known since she was a puppy. These are particularly strong attachments. For example, she absolutely loves the woman who lives one house uphill from us, the man who lives one house downhill from us, my mother-in-law, and some neighborhood dogs she has known since she was small. It is sad

CHAPTER 5. OTHER SURPRISES

though, because, for example, she has a dog friend Otis, who is a Chocolate Labrador she has known for four years. Sadly, Otis is 12 years old, and not long for this world. She used to often say hello to Otis through gaps in his brick fence. She speeds up if I mention that we will walk past Otis' house, but Otis is getting so old now that we see him only once or twice every month, instead of a couple of times a week. Otis now walks with stiff legs, but he speeds up when he sees Hazel at the park or in the street, because he is keen to say hello. Hazel is not going to understand when Otis dies.

I am surprised that Hazel responds immediately if a stranger walking towards us in the street smiles at her. She starts wagging her tail, thinking she will get a pat. If it is someone off the confrontation line who is smiling at her, she will plant her feet, chin up with tail wagging, waiting for me to go to them, or for them to come to us. One young female university student said "that made my day" after Hazel picked her out and stared at her, head up, tail wagging vigorously and waited for her to come over to pat her; it was during the university's final exam period, and I think the poor girl was stressed out.

I am surprised at how disappointed and confused Hazel is when she stops to wag her tail at a passing stranger, but that person walks past *without* patting her. It is, however, a short-lived problem; she quickly moves on to pick out another "victim."

Hazel has a couple of women friends who dote on her, and both have in common that they use lemon-scented hand cream. I was surprised that my wife knows immediately that Hazel has seen one of those women when Hazel comes home, because her fur holds the scent for a few hours. It is a tell-tale sign of Hazel's infidelity, like lipstick on the collar.

I have ten times as many social interactions with people in the street since I got a dog. I talk to the neighbors much more than I used to. Complete strangers stop me in the street 100 times more often than they used to. If I were single, Hazel would be a great ice-breaker. A woman at work described Hazel as a "chick magnet," and admitted having met her own partner at the dog park. In my case, my Hazel's many efforts to introduce me to attractive young women are wasted, because I am firmly married. I do wonder, however, how many marriages have been wrecked because of a dog picking out a new wife or husband.

I have seen the same guy at the bus stop 100+ times in the last 10 years. He must be about 80

CHAPTER 5. OTHER SURPRISES

years old now. We always nod and say hello, and share a few words. One day, I met him while walking Hazel, and he patted her. I was surprised, however, that he patted her like he had never patted a dog before. I found it odd that someone of that advanced age, with full mental faculties, did not know how to pat a dog. Ignorance about dogs is much more common with young people, and with foreign people. In those cases, I show them how to stroke Hazel and I tell them what she likes (e.g., tickle her under the chin and scratch her chest, etc.).

After more than four years with Hazel, I am amazed that Labradors are used as guide dogs for the blind. Sure enough, they have a good temperament and a reasonable intelligence, but Hazel is so curious about so many distractions that I think she would have flunked out of guide dog training school; I guess many dogs *do* flunk out.

I was surprised that when I pick up our cat, Hazel goes crazy, trying to get the cat. I read that perhaps it is something to do with the cat being at a higher level, and seeming a threat. On the other hand, Hazel does not care if the cat is above her on a piece of furniture when the cat is *not* being held. I also read that picking up the cat is like picking up a toy, and your dog thinks it is a game and gets suddenly interested and excited. Similarly, if I pick up one of our pet rabbits while Hazel is nearby, Hazel gets very excited, and tries jumping up on me, as if she thinks I am bringing her a tasty treat.

I was surprised to find that when Hazel pulls over to sniff at something, like a hedge on the corner of a street, or something unsavory in the grass, I can feel her sniffing through the lead. That is, when the lead is pulled taut, and she is rapidly sniffing in and out, I feel that vibration transmitted all the way through the taut lead; it is unmistakable.

I was surprised that my dark Chocolate Labrador started to get a grey/white chin at only two-and-a-half years of age. Some folks call it "sugar face." It is a sign of aging, and I mistakenly thought it would happen much later than that.

At age four, I discovered that Hazel has a "Henry's pocket" ear skin fold. What is that for?

Nobody told us that dogs have seasonal moods. I was surprised that although Hazel is "fixed," she still gets "spring fever." When spring arrives, she is bouncy and like a puppy again. She is pulling at the lead again, although we trained her out of it. At the park I tell her to sit, while I walk away, as part of her training, which she does, but in spring she whines because she wants to start running to chase

CHAPTER 5. OTHER SURPRISES

the ball I have not even thrown yet. She meets new people and acts like she drank six cups of coffee. She runs and runs until she drops. Maybe it is because the sun is rising earlier, there are more birds tweeting, the flowers are more fragrant, the rabbits are running around, it is warm enough to swim in the ocean again, and it all excites her. On the other hand, in the depths of winter, Hazel starts to get a little reluctant to obey commands. She might hesitate before sitting or coming, etc. So, we use a slightly sterner voice and we reinforce some of the commands with higher-value rewards. I think she is just having a little less fun in the colder months, with shorter days, and perhaps fewer smells to sniff.

Sometimes I make Hazel sit until I have thrown a ball for her at the park, and other times I let her anticipate and run off in the direction she thinks the ball will go. I am surprised that while Hazel is running in anticipation of me throwing the ball, if I throw the ball slightly to the left or right of the line she is running on, 30 yards (30 metres) from where I am standing, she will hear it whishing through the air before it actually passes her, and without looking up or seeing it, she will alter course to intercept it. Perhaps this is some inherent gun dog or bird dog genetic Retriever trait.

When Hazel retrieves a tennis ball at the park and drops it at my feet, I was at first surprised that I have to put my foot on it as I am giving her a treat. Otherwise, she eats her treat and immediately grabs the ball off the ground and runs off with it before I can throw it again.

I am surprised that little dogs that weigh one-tenth of what Hazel weighs routinely try to start fights with her, barking at her and straining at their leads trying to get her in the street. What are they trying to prove? She never starts a fight with a random small dog, but boy does she get riled up if one barks at her. As mentioned elsewhere, we are actively and successfully training Hazel to tone down her response, both to arch-enemy dogs and to random small dogs that bark at her.

I was surprised that my gentle carefree floppy-eared Silly-Billy good-with-children good-with-old-people cute dog who loves everybody will suddenly turn on a dime and become aggressive, barking like a wolf if another dog barks at her, or if she sees an arch-enemy dog, or if she sees an unusual human. This instant flip-of-a-switch change in her demeanor is a reminder that her wolf ancestors are not that many generations up the family tree. Given this, I am never surprised when I hear that someone with

CHAPTER 5. OTHER SURPRISES

a dangerous exotic pet gets mauled or killed by it.

Hazel is confused by things that she does not understand. She can get aggressive when she is confused. For example, we were sitting at a bench in the central city, and a elderly man in a long white robe (maybe a Middle-Eastern kaftan) stopped on the other side of the street, and then started to cross the street slowly towards us. He was walking with the aid of a metal walking frame with wheels. He had his head down, and I do not think he even saw us. Hazel stopped and stared with 100% attention. Then as he got closer, she started growling and went wild, raring up and barking very loudly and aggressively. I think it was a combination of the long white robe, the walking frame, the slow plodding approach, and the fact that he was walking straight at us with his head down.

Similarly, I was surprised that Hazel became grumpy and aggressive when a lady was walking a wheelbarrow towards us on a narrow grassy path. Again, it was a stranger with a strange wheeled device, walking head-down towards us. In that case, Hazel made a few low guttural warning growls and then started raring up and barking at her. I should have stopped Hazel when she started her guttural growls, by holding her snout and/or talking her down. However, the woman looked a little entertained (and she could see that Hazel was a Labrador and that I was not some villain). Instead, I let it play out, out of curiosity. I will not let her do that again, if I can help it.

Another day, we stopped to say hello to an old man who lives down the street from us. He calls Hazel "Cocoa" because of her color. He is at least 90 years old. As he was talking, he bent over to give her a pat, but he stumbled very slightly, and she almost jumped out of her skin. Even though Hazel knows him, and had met him 10 times in exactly the same spot, the unusual sudden stumble spooked her; I thought she might bark, but I calmed her with soft words, and she settled down quickly. Hazel also jumps if a nearby flag (of the sort used for advertisements at street level) suddenly flaps in the wind.

I was surprised the first time that I walked through a grassy tree-filled domain in front of our city museum and Hazel saw people sitting down on the grass talking. Whenever she sees people sitting down in grassy areas, often a young person on their own, or a young couple, she stops, plants her feet, wags her tail, and wants to go over to say hello. If they beckon for her, I bring her over, otherwise

CHAPTER 5. OTHER SURPRISES

not. One girl whipped out her cell phone and took a photo of Hazel because she seemed so attentive. I think that when she sees people down on her level, she assumes that they are there to play with her. The same thing often happens if I lie down on the carpet at home to do a stretch; she typically comes over and tries to lick my face or she flops down beside me and sits one paw on me.

I am amazed at how food-driven Hazel's behavior is. She is always looking for something to eat. For example, I prepare a "Kong" for her every day. (It is an excellent sturdy hollow rubber chew toy, shaped like a snowman, and coming in different colors and different grades of strength.) I often put a few frozen green peas in it, along with possum meat, carrots, rice cakes, etc. I cut out a carrot stopper for the narrow end, and then I add water and freeze it. Hazel always comes and watches me making it. I always "accidentally" drop a couple of frozen green peas, saying "Ooops!," and she charges after them. I am surprised that she will get up out of her comfy chair, or come from a distant room, and come to the kitchen, just to get a couple of frozen green peas.

I was surprised by how different dogs' appetites can be. I met a guy at the park who said that his Labrador had once gotten increasingly overweight and then become obese, and at the time he had no idea why. He eventually figured out that, through lack of communication, his wife had been feeding their dog whenever it was hungry. It took ages to get the dog back to a healthy weight. On the other hand, the elderly woman across the street from us has a little dog who has no appetite; she says it eats once a day, and is not really interested in food or eating. It must be difficult to train a dog with no appetite.

I am surprised by how useful Hazel is when I am walking up a steep hill. It is often wet grass, muddy, and uneven ground. I shout out "mush, mush!" and Hazel helps to pull me up the hill. I also use her, via her lead, as an anchor when walking on hilly terrain. If I am walking sideways across a steep hillside, I have her on the up-hill side of me, and I pull her rear harness lead as if I am trying to lift her off the ground. That dog/anchor provides wonderful stability on an uneven surface. Note, however, that this would not work at all if she were on the down-hill side, in which case pulling the lead would destabilize me. Also, these actions would not work with a small/light dog.

I am surprised by how quickly Hazel falls into a deep REM sleep dream state. In humans, I think

CHAPTER 5. OTHER SURPRISES

it takes about 90 minutes to reach this stage, but Hazel is often there in five or 10 minutes.

I was surprised by how *vivid* Hazel's dreams must be. Some of them are good dreams, but some of them are bad dreams. She will be sound asleep, but her legs and feet will start twitching in unison, as if she is running, and she will make all sorts of dog noises (growling, suppressed barking, suppressed guttural yelps, etc.). If she is curled up on my lap and dreaming of running, I can feel her whole body moving. Sometimes she dreams she is drinking, and you can see her mouth moving and swallowing. Sometimes she dreams she is eating, and you see her chewing and swallowing. We see this every day, and it is amusing. I wish we had some sort of telepathic dog dream-o-vision we could project on the television screen to see what she is dreaming about. I have been tempted to wake her during bad dreams, but have never done so because we worry about triggering her dyskinesia (discussed next). She sometimes looks a little confused when she wakes from a vivid dream.

Hazel suffers from "paroxysmal dyskinesia." It is relatively common in Labradors. "Paroxysmal" is Greek for "every now and then," "dys" is Greek for abnormal or difficult, and "kinesia" is Greek for movement. So, "paroxysmal dyskinesia" means every now and then having difficulty with movement. If Hazel has had a really good run the park (or a strenuous hill walk) within the last 24 hours, and is deeply asleep, and someone knocks on the front door (or some other sharp noise occurs) then she suddenly springs to her feet, barks a warning, bounds along looking fine for 10–20 seconds, but then her feet start make clumping/thumping sounds as she plods oddly, then she walks in a small circle like she has rabies, and then she drops to the ground. She clamps her mouth tightly shut (so her baggy Labrador jowls disappear completely), tucks her tail between her back legs, her eyes grow wide and glassy, and she looks frightened and confused, because she can only lie on her side, and she cannot walk. Her head and upper body begin to shake. Sometimes she also makes mild whining noises.

We comfort Hazel and it passes in maybe five minutes, or a little longer. She is very tired afterwards. It happens, on average, about once every month. There have been a couple of times when she did not seem to be deeply asleep just before it happened, but maybe she was just very relaxed or dozing, or maybe we did not notice the depth of her sleep.

CHAPTER 5. OTHER SURPRISES

We liken her dyskinesia to human sleep paralysis, which can happen during a transition from sleeping to waking (or vice versa) when you are conscious but cannot move. When you are asleep, your brain has to turn off the movement signals, else you would actually be running when you dream that you are running. In Hazel's case, turning the signals back on again does not always go smoothly when she wakes suddenly from a deep sleep.

Hazel's dyskinesia episodes (we incorrectly refer loosely to them at home as "seizures") have only ever happened at home when she jumps up after being asleep or relaxed. We have never met a vet who has heard of this condition, but YouTube has dozens of videos of Labradors having dyskinesia episodes.

I have not yet seen any YouTube videos that describe dyskinesia as being related to the asleep-awake transition. In some of the videos, the dog having the seizure was outside and active when it happened—but those cases might instead have been canine epilepsy. (There is some confusion over dog seizures, and we are not experts.) Out of an abundance of caution, however, we are cautious when Hazel is swimming in the ocean. We make a point of not throwing a stick too far out in the water for her to retrieve, because we need to be able to rescue her quickly if she has a dyskinesia episode, to prevent her drowning.

When Hazel goes to sleep on my lap, I can feel her heart beat against my abdomen. It surprises me that the rhythm of her heart is so very different from a human heart rhythm.

I am surprised that Hazel follows us around the house. She often settles in my home office when I am working, then settles in the living room if I am watching TV, sits on the big chair in the dining room if we are eating at the table, etc. I think she just wants to be with the "pack." One consequence of her following us around is that I am surprised by the number of times that Hazel gets underfoot in the house, almost tripping us over.

Hazel constantly begs for food during meal preparation. You cannot leave food unattended and in reach for even a moment. For her first 6–9 months, Hazel would bark and whine while food was being prepared. She still does it a little, even at age four years, especially if we are cooking her favorite human foods (e.g., pasta). We have trained her to sit outside the kitchen, behind a wooden concertina gate I installed. She quickly learned, however, how to open the concertina gate with her nose. So, I had

CHAPTER 5. OTHER SURPRISES

to make and install a locking mechanism to prevent that. We also had to put a bar stool in front of one end of the gate to stop her trying to overcome the first locking mechanism.

I am surprised that Hazel likes cushions. She will move a cushion on a sofa to a favored position, then circle it several times, pawing it into the ideal position, before flopping down with her head and one paw on it.

Dogs sense warmth. So, unless you teach your dog otherwise, when you get up off the sofa to go to get a drink, you will come back to find the dog curled up where you were sitting. I usually pick up her and her cushion and shunt her over to the other end of the sofa. Hazel will even go to the door, pretending to want to go out, just so that she can jump into your chair when you go to open the door for her. She also jumps up onto the bed where my torso was when I get up in the morning.

I know that dogs have good noses, but I was surprised when walking in the city once that Hazel stopped and showed a particular interest in a parking lot behind a low fence. To humor her, I walked over and let her follow whatever it was that piqued her sense of smell. I could see nothing, but about 20 paces away, someone had dropped some peanuts in the parking lot. She headed directly for them.

Similarly, I am surprised that she will be snoozing inside in the front room, and then suddenly jump up barking and head for the back door, 30 feet (10 metres) away through a hallway and into another room. If we let her out and follow her, there will be a hedgehog in the back yard 20 feet (6 metres) from the back door, or there is one over the neighbor's fence in *their* back yard. Somehow she smelled it far from the back door, from inside, while asleep, three rooms away from the back door.

I am surprised at how physically inflexible Hazel is. She cannot turn her head far to either side. Similarly, her back legs move only in certain planes, etc. It is reassuring to think that if you are attacked by a dog, they are not terribly flexible.

Hazel once did a massive, truly massive, half soft-serve poo in the street in the central city. It was impossible to clean up completely. A nice lady walking by commented on it and commiserated with me. She mentioned that her 13-year old dog had recently had an injection for arthritis that was meant to make her dog happier, but her dog had gone downhill rapidly and she had spent a month trying to nurse the dog back to good health. She said that she had a trip planned in a couple of weeks and was

CHAPTER 5. OTHER SURPRISES

fearful of leaving the dog in someone else's care in that state. Just as it took time and effort to care for a new puppy, it takes time and effort to care for an elderly dog.

I was surprised that although Hazel ignores seagulls, blackbirds, sparrows, herons, cormorants, oystercatchers, etc., she goes absolutely ballistic if she scents a city pigeon. There is one spot in the city, right outside the Psychiatric Services wing of the local Public Hospital where pigeons love to sit on the grass and on the window sills. She starts bounding along in anticipation of this spot about a 100 yards (100 metres) before we get there. Then, if she does not get there fast enough for her liking she starts pining/whining. Sometimes, she makes so much noise trying to get to the pigeons that we attract attention from someone on an upper hospital floor; I just give them a wave. Some bemused passersby were curious and I told them she just loves pigeons. Some other passersby are terrified of this running dark animal, clearly intent on getting something. Nobody is in any danger, but sometimes she looks really scary.

I am surprised by how often Hazel loses her tennis ball at the park. I often take two with me, just in case. I am similarly surprised by how often I *find* a tennis ball at the park. It is no good buying just one tennis ball for your dog, because it can lose that the first time you play with it. Losing balls may be partly related to dog vision, discussed next.

I am surprised by Hazel's vision. At the park, she has difficulty finding a yellow tennis ball on the green grass (I think that they both look yellow to her). Apparently, however, dogs can perceive more shades of blue than humans can. In the garden at night, however, her eyesight is much better than mine. Apparently, dog's have larger pupils than humans and, unlike humans, their eyes are dominated by "rod" cells, that work well at night. Their visual acuity (i.e., ability to see details) is, however, much worse than humans; they also have worse depth perception than humans, because the fields of vision from their eyes overlap much less than in humans (Rao, 2021).

I was walking Hazel through the central city, and a little girl, aged maybe seven or eight, called out "can I pat your dog?" He mother was a few yards (metres) away, watching and nodding. So, I said "yes." The girl asked Hazel's name and age, and then she asked a question that surprised me: "What is her favorite color?" I thought about it and answered "blue," telling the girl that dogs see

CHAPTER 5. OTHER SURPRISES

more shades of blue than we do.

When I had family members in hospital, I was surprised that two local hospitals were perfectly happy to have Hazel come in to visit patients in the wards. One of the Hospitals said "yes" without even asking her breed or her nature. I doubt that they would have agreed so readily in the U.S., because of litigation risk (if she bit someone). In New Zealand, however, it is almost impossible to sue anyone for that sort of incident (or, indeed, for almost anything). So, I think they did not worry about it.

As I was leaving after one hospital visit, but while still in the hospital building, a young woman came rushing over to see Hazel. She said that her father had died in the hospital that morning, and she needed to pat Hazel to cheer herself up. Hazel leant against the young woman and shook hands/paws with her several times, and Hazel sat on the young woman's feet, which the young woman thought was funny. The young woman asked for some kibble to give Hazel, which I happily handed over. Hazel licked her face, and the young woman seemed slightly comforted.

Another day, I took Hazel to visit my mother in hospital. Unbeknownst to me, my mother had been moved since the previous day. So, I had to walk around the ward to find her. While walking around, a woman spotted Hazel and called out to me, asking if Hazel could come and see her father. I said "sure thing." I walked Hazel over to a bed with a big curtain all the way around it. The woman directed me behind the curtain. There was a man in bed, aged maybe 70, hooked up to a breathing tube and some monitors. A gray-haired woman, presumably his wife, was sitting in a chair beside the bed. He had clearly had a stroke, and was relatively unresponsive. The wife told the man that there was a dog here to see him, and Hazel came over and put her front paws up on the bed. The wife guided the man's arm over towards Hazel's head and his eyes followed his hand. The wife was very excited and said seeing his eyes move was the most response they had seen all day (and it was 5PM already). Then the man gave a half smile as Hazel licked his hand and he touched her. The wife and daughter were ecstatic at this even greater response. I could see that Hazel wanted to jump up on the bed, but I held her harness and stopped her. We stayed for a couple of minutes, and then said our goodbyes and went off to find my mother.

Many people find Hazel very comforting. We

CHAPTER 5. OTHER SURPRISES

think that is partly because she is an attractive pure-bred dog and is genetically bred to be good around people, and partly because she has been well socialized by us. So, her behavior is a mix of nature and nurture. In contrast, if you start with a rescue dog, and you do not (or can not) put in the effort to train your dog, then I think that the outcome will be much more uncertain.

Chapter 6

We Learned the Hard Way

This chapter focuses on experiences where we (or someone else) made a mistake and learned from it. We hope that you can avoid the same mistakes.

Hazel loves to run with other dogs, or chase a ball and retrieve it at the park. She is a great sprinter, but unlike, say, a Border Collie or a Vizsla, Hazel reaches a point where after five minutes of intense exercise, she overheats and drops to the ground. She seeks shady, damp/cool grass, and stretches out on her belly to cool down, while she puffs and pants. It is especially bad on a warm or

CHAPTER 6. WE LEARNED THE HARD WAY

sunny day, but still happens even in the dead of winter, though to a much lesser extent.

I was surprised the first time that Hazel flopped in a complete collapse on the cool grass and refused to budge. Now, when she does it, I give her a few belly rubs, and tell her that we will go sit on a park bench, and I point at the bench. Then, she jumps to her feet and we go and sit on the park bench in the shade. She sits there panting, and it takes her 10 minutes to cool off and get her breath back.

On one park visit, Hazel ran in big circles with a dog we know, and then I tried to get her to walk over to a park bench to sit down, and she dropped to the ground two or three times on the way over. When we got there, she sat on the bench beside me, but after a minute started leaning on me, and then flopped onto my lap, with me holding her head. She panted for 15 minutes before we could walk the 500 yards (500 metres) back up the hill to our house. She was still panting a little at the house.

I should have stopped her sooner; her little dog brain overestimated her energy level, and so did I. That was too much exercise, and I learned the hard way that I should have been more careful with her, especially on a warm day. Nowadays I regulate her exercise, stopping her early, even when she is having a good time with one of her best dog friends. She may be disappointed when I stop her play on a warm day, but I think it is in her best interest for me to not let her get exhausted.

When it was time for a walk, I used to just open the front gate and step out onto the sidewalk with Hazel. I stopped doing that when we were surprised to meet another dog right outside our front gate, and Hazel went ballistic, raring up on her hind legs and barking like a wolf. Perhaps Hazel became aggressive because she views our gate as the entry to our property, and she felt very defensive of our home. Nowadays, I always stick my head out into the street over the front gate, and look both ways. If anyone is coming, I wait until they are long gone before going out—unless it is one of her human or dog friends.

I have also been surprised that if the cat is in the front yard when Hazel and I go for a walk, the cat sometimes follows us. We turn back and try to convince the cat to stay home. Sometimes I grab the cat and carry it back indoors, but Hazel goes ballistic when I pick up the cat in the street.

I always take at least three doggy poo bags with me on a dog walk. That need surprised me. Most of the time, however, I use only one bag. Sometimes,

CHAPTER 6. WE LEARNED THE HARD WAY

especially if Hazel has been unwell, I need two or three bags for her. It is also good to have one extra bag, in case I want to pick up some other dog's poo after having already put Hazel's poo in the garbage can. It is also good to have an extra poo bag for the rare occasions where you put your hand in the empty poo bag, like putting on a glove, and your hand goes right through the bag, because the bag is badly made and was not crimped properly.

I was surprised that when I pick up a poo with a doggy poo bag, it still smells bad. The bag reduces the smell by 90%, but a fresh dog poo smells so strongly that you can still smell it through the bag. At first, we carried a little Tupperware container to put the poo bag into, but that was a bad idea (for hygiene and convenience reasons). Now, I tie the bag to the clip on the lead until I get to a garbage can. I may have to carry that stinking poo for 10 minutes until I actually find a garbage can.

I am surprised by how difficult it is to open doggy poo bags when using them, especially on a cold day when wearing gloves. Static electricity holds the plastic bag closed. I often open a bag at home and scrunch it up a little, before putting it in my pocket, to make it easier to open when needed, otherwise I can be stuck standing there beside a stinking fresh poo on the ground, with my fingers going numb while I try to open some bag I cannot even feel, while Hazel is raring to go and straining at the lead. I have the same difficulty opening plastic bags for produce in the supermarket; if you rub the opening-end of the bag between your hands, however, it can help to open it up.

I was surprised that when I meet another dog owner in the street or the park, and we are both walking our dogs on leads, and we stop to talk, the dogs often start circling each other, and their leads get crossed. The crossed leads can tie the two dogs together, which is a bad thing if any aggression breaks out. So, nowadays I am more careful. I pull Hazel back a bit to stop her circling. Sometimes, I start to circle too, and the other dog owner has no choice but to do the same to avoid me. Often, however, the other dog owner will counter by purposely dropping their lead, not noticing that I am already pulling Hazel back to prevent a lead tangle.

To start with, we used a single lead attached to a single D-ring on Hazel's collar. It was not working; Hazel is too strong and we had no control. So, we quickly adopted a two-point harness. One lead clips onto a D-ring on her harness at the middle of her back and the other lead clips on to a D-ring on

CHAPTER 6. WE LEARNED THE HARD WAY

her harness on her chest. In the middle of the lead is a free hanging loop clipped to a ring that floats between the two lead clips.

The two-point harness means that Hazel is not being choked if she pulls at her lead. (I see many other eager dogs choking themselves when they pull at their lead; it looks and sounds awful.) Also, when used as a three-foot (one metre) lead with two clips, I can hold the handle with one hand and slip my other hand into the V of the double-point lead. This gives me a two-handed grip on her, which is very useful if I need to exert extra control. If I unclip one clip, then the lead can double from about three feet (one metre) to about six feet (two metres). The longer lead is good when we go for a short run at the beach. I am surprised to see that 99% of dog owners in my city do not use a two-point harness. However, I would never do it any other way now, because we avoid choking her and it gives me two-handed control of a good-sized strong dog.

My wife was baking a French pear/almond tart to bring to a social event that evening. Hazel (following the smell?) jumped up at the oven when my wife was out of the room and her paw flipped the controls and added 100 degrees to the oven temperature. (It is a SMEG electric oven with flipper controls.) The tart was wrecked in 10 minutes. We had to rush to the store to get more pears to make another. Oven controls that Hazel can operate present a fire risk. So, we now monitor cooking more carefully, use a concertina gate to block entry to the kitchen, and we turn the oven off at the wall after each use, all of which are a hassle. If your oven has knobs rather than levers, then this will be much less of an issue.

We were staying at a holiday home, and we were keeping Hazel's food supplies in a bag behind the closed bathroom door. We did not pay too much attention to that room, because the sliding door was supposed to be closed all the time. I was surprised, however, to see Hazel walking out of that room one evening, licking her chops. Someone had left the sliding door ajar, and Hazel must have slid it open with her nose. At first, I thought she had gotten into her food supply. In fact, she had gone in and been unable to get into the bag holding her food and had instead munched on a bar of soap. It had her teeth marks in it, but she had eaten very little. I think she did not like it. Fortunately, it was a natural no-added-chemical soap, and the quantity consumed was small. So, she was not sick. We gave her a big drink of water, and we made a point of

CHAPTER 6. WE LEARNED THE HARD WAY

making sure that the soap (and everything else in there) was out of her reach from then on.

Once, we came back from an overnight trip and our bags were sitting on the floor, unzipped. Four-year old Hazel had a moment alone with one bag and pulled out a natural deodorant (made with magnesium hydroxide, coconut oil, etc., in a cardboard push tube). She managed to eat half of it before she was discovered. It likely tasted like coconut-flavored white chocolate to her. Google said nothing in the ingredients was toxic, and that the likely outcome was diarrhea. In fact, nothing unusual happened. I guess that we were relaxed after our trip, and we dropped our guard for a minute; lesson learned.

My daughter told me about "happy tail syndrome." It is when a dog wags its tail very much and accidentally hits something with its tail and splits its tail open. A split tail is a difficult thing to heal, partly because it can be easily injured again, and partly because the dog can reach the injury with its mouth, and chew at any bandage. We think that Hazel is at risk of suffering from happy tail syndrome. She is a sturdy animal, and has good fur coverage on her tail, but gosh she makes loud whacking sounds often, when her tail hits walls or doors, etc. Once she did this outside my office door while I was talking to someone, and the person in the office next door opened the door, thinking someone was knocking. Nowadays, I usually step between her and the thing her tail is hitting, to cushion the blows and reduce this risk.

Hazel enjoys playing fetch at the park. We have decided, however, to limit how often we play fetch with her. Although Labradors are Gun Dogs, the sudden burst of sprinting and the rapid changes in direction when running are not good for joints or bones, and many dogs have been injured this way. Retrieving a tennis ball is not like jumping into a lake and swimming over to a dead duck and bringing it back; instead, it is much more jarring to a dog's body. Hazel has never showed any signs of joint injury, but that is likely a long-term effect that we would not see for several years. The bottom line is that we have consciously chosen to reduce the frequency and intensity of playing fetch with Hazel.

Here is an awful/embarrassing experience that reduced our trust in our dog. Hazel is a Labrador Retriever. She was bred as a Gun Dog. As mentioned elsewhere, I regularly take her to the park, unleash her, tell her to sit, walk away a few paces, throw a tennis ball a good distance with a ball-

CHAPTER 6. WE LEARNED THE HARD WAY

throwing stick, and let her run after it, and bring it back. When she drops it at my feet, often with the command "Drop!," she gets a bit of kibble to eat.

However, one summer day while playing fetch Hazel was returning to me with the ball on her second run when she dropped the ball 10 yards (10 metres) away and veered off away from me, up a small hill in the park, off to my right. I had my back to the nearby park entrance and had not noticed that a man was walking by with two dogs, one light and one dark.

I had seen him many times before, at exactly that spot, with those same two dogs. I knew which house he lived in nearby. My wife had warned me about his dark dog being aggressive, because Hazel had met it three years earlier when Hazel was still a puppy. Hazel had wanted to play, but the dark dog had growled at her and Hazel had given up, confused and scared.

As a more mature dog, however, Hazel does not like being growled at, and she wants to defend herself (and family members). On this day, Hazel ran over to this same dog, probably just to play, but I think it growled at her again, and she was in no mood to back down. The dark dog was being walked off-lead, so the owner could not pull it out of the way. Hazel jumped very aggressively on the dark dog and was hovering over it in a domineering way, with lots of barking and thrashing about. The other dog flipped over in submission, and I think Hazel was mouthing its belly (Labradors have a soft bite, and can mouth things without actually biting).

I started sprinting over to the conflict zone before Hazel even got to the dog, because I recognized the man and his awful dog. I got there mid-conflict and pulled Hazel's body harness to wrench her out of the fight. (This is another good reason to have a harness in place of a collar; I have done the same to another larger dog on a different occasion when it was doing the same to a different small dog.) The small dark dog was shaken but not injured. The man walking the dog was horrified and indignant and asked for my details and for Hazel's registration number, which I gave, with many apologies.

To any outside observer (and, unfortunately, there was one walking towards that very spot at that very moment) it must have looked like an evil wolf viciously attacking an innocent rabbit. The man told me that his dog was 16 years old and deaf. To the observer walking by who heard this, Hazel must have appeared to be a poorly-trained monster.

CHAPTER 6. WE LEARNED THE HARD WAY

My wife told me later that on the previous occasion, three years earlier, when the other dog had growled at Hazel and Hazel had backed away, the owner had told her that his dog is often attacked by other dogs. I deduced that he was walking it off-lead because it was not properly trained to walk on-lead, and not properly trained in general.

The end result is that we no longer completely trust Hazel to run off-lead at the park when playing fetch. We think she is getting too excited by the explosive energy of the fetch experience, and getting too worked up, and that this can boost her usually-mild level of aggressiveness. Also, we think that playing fetch is cultivating a prey instinct that Labradors do not naturally have.

So, now I let Hazel off lead to play fetch in an open space only if there are no other dogs anywhere nearby and little or no chance of other dogs surprising us. I choose open spaces with good sight lines to any entry point to the area, and I look around often, before, during, and after throwing the ball. We do still play fetch, but less often, less intensely, and only when the coast is clear—and almost never at that original park near the house of the man with the dark dog. Hazel is, however, still allowed off-lead at other parks, to run around with a pack of

5–10 dogs who are there to play, and that activity typically does not involve retrieving.

I mentioned previously that violent dog encounters are just part of the dog ownership experience. In over 1,000 days with Hazel, the example just given is the only time she has made aggressive physical contact with another dog. Thus, on 99.9% of our days with her, she has not behaved this way. We are lucky that the victim did not make a formal complaint. In practice, however, even if he had complained, we would likely only have gotten a mild warning, if that. I think that only if your dog attacks other dogs many times with many complaints will you be forced to have the dog put down or to pay compensation to another dog owner. Of course, if your dog attacks a human, then your dog could be subject to destruction immediately.

I was surprised that Hazel gets bored of going to the same park all the time (the one that is a short walk from our house). When we go anywhere new, however, she charges ahead almost running (on the lead) to explore, because she is excited by the new experience. So, even though chasing a ball at the park or just walking around the park is kind of mindless and she enjoys it, she very much enjoys walking in a *new* neighborhood or going to a *new*

CHAPTER 6. WE LEARNED THE HARD WAY

park or a *different* beach. Her dog brain may be only 100 grams (compared with 1,200–1,400 grams for a human brain), but she still actively seeks out and enjoys new environments.

Play dates between your dog and other dogs might be pre-arranged by you (we do that maybe 1% of the time) or just by happenstance (the other 99% of the time in our case). We know, for example, that at 4:30PM at one local park, we are likely to find 5–10 friendly dogs; other people know that too, and so dogs being there to play is a self-fulfilling prophecy. It took us a while to figure out where the local dog hotspots are. If we were just starting out our first-dog experience, we would stop another dog owner in the street and ask for guidance.

One evening, Hazel jumped up super-excited and ran to the back door, woofing and wanting desperately to go out. She stuck her snout out the cat flap and was whining to go out. When I opened the door, she rushed out so hard and so quickly that she stumbled, face-planting on the door mat and scraping her wrist on the brick paving outside my back door. We noticed later that she had grazed her wrist and taken a small eighth-of-an-inch-square (3mm-square) divot out of her fur.

I was surprised that Hazel's fur coat did not

protect her from falling only six inches. I guess that her rushing speed was the problem, and/or that she caught the edge of one brick. I think she was after a hedgehog. Nowadays, I am more cautious when she is overly eager to get out. I try to make sure that she does not stumble out of the door, either by not letting her out in the first place until she calms down, or by letting her out in a more controlled manner, or shining a flashlight just outside the back door to improve visibility.

Hazel had a similar stumble at the park once, when she was running to jump over a very low wooden hurdle, and she clipped it with her front leg and when flying, sprawled sideways, and spinning like an ice-hockey player who had been body-checked. She was sore and limping a little for a few days. This stumbling may tie in with the general lack of visual depth perception in dogs mentioned earlier.

Dog "crates" are a complicated issue. They are certainly popular. Many people told us we "needed" to use one to train Hazel, even though "crate training" has only existed since the 1980's, mainly in the U.S., and before that nobody used them! They appear to be illegal in Sweden and very unpopular in Europe and Australia. We bought one and it was a

CHAPTER 6. WE LEARNED THE HARD WAY

disaster, partly because we were not familiar with dogs and puppy "language," and so we did not use it correctly, with positive reinforcement and gradual adjustment. We gave up on it after a few nights of pitiful howling and we let Hazel sleep in a dog bed in our room, which has worked out fine. We regret buying a crate.

We think the main reason people "crate" their dogs is to keep them contained while they are at work—to stop their dog destroying an empty house. Luckily, one of us is almost always home during the day. So, this has never been an issue for us. Many people only crate dogs as puppies, but not when they are older and more settled.

At one estuary spot, when the tide is low, the water is only 30 feet (10 metres) wide to cross, to get to a sandy area in the middle of the estuary, but when the tide is high, it is a half-mile (800 metres) across. At high tide, we have taken Hazel on a "swim-walk" there. With her lead on, but double length, we walk into the water. She walks at first, and then swims. She can swim very quickly, with her big webbed flipper feet, so we have to pull her back a bit. We figured out on an earlier occasion that Hazel wanted to just keep going when not on a lead, and to try to swim to the other side. At high tide, however, that would exhaust her. So, we keep her on a lead at those times now.

Hazel does not like it when small dogs who are not her friends yap at her. She tends to bark back at them raring up her hind legs and straining at the lead. After several cases of this, we started doing intense "quiet puppy" training in the street—as well as in the kitchen. So, we praise her and reward her with kibble for being quiet around other dogs, and doubly so for small dogs that bark at her. I will get her to go to one side of the sidewalk, maybe a couple of paces up a driveway, or slightly out into a quiet street, and get her to sit when noisy little dogs are approaching. Then I say "shuuush" with my finger to my lips and say "quiet puppy" and give her a treat if she is quiet and keep doing that until noisy dogs have passed. If she barks at them, she gets no treat. Sometimes, I can tell she is about to bark, and I hold her snout closed. The training is working very well, with a clear improvement. Most recently, she is purposely being quiet when small dogs yap at her, and then looking to me for her treat.

I was surprised that Hazel does not always learn her lesson. For example, she was chewing on a stick and bit off a piece that got jammed horizontally

CHAPTER 6. WE LEARNED THE HARD WAY

between her upper back teeth. She was shaking her head around like crazy and walking backwards and retching and trying to get it out. Once I figured out the problem, I opened her mouth, reached in and pulled it out. I showed it to her and told her not to do that again, but she grabbed it instantly from my hand and put it in her mouth again! Now, when I pull something out of her mouth, I do not show it to her, for fear she will snatch it.

On that note, sometimes you get a scare. Hazel came home from a walk and was dribbling almost uncontrollably. She was slurping it up and swallowing a lot, and leaving a dribble pool on the carpet. That means either there is something stuck in her mouth, or she has been poisoned (likely by eating something on a walk she should not have eaten). We looked in her mouth with a flashlight but could see nothing. I looked several times and felt about with my fingers. My wife was on the phone to the vet, worried about poison, when I finally spotted it. She had been chewing sticks and had a small sliver of wood between two rear teeth, and it was pushing up into her gum. I tried a toothpick, but I could not get enough leverage. I have a set of stainless steel dental tools in one of my tool bags, so I chose a hooked pick and held her down on her side with her head on its side on a cushion, and picked it out. It would not have been possible without a slender metal tool; I am not sure what I would have used without the dental tools. It took a couple of hours for Hazel to return to normal and to stop salivating. Ask yourself right now what tool you have that is like a dentist's pick; you may need one.

I am surprised that owners of smaller dogs compliment me on how good Hazel's teeth look. We think that it is mostly because she chews sticks, that, basically, act like toothpicks. Small dog's jaws are not, however, strong enough to munch down a piece of tree branch. We think that small dogs get more dental problems than big dogs as a result. Sometimes when walking in the bush, Hazel does what my wife refers to as "lumberjacking," where she puts her head sideways and chews on a young tree until it falls down; it looks like a beaver did it. (Obviously, we would not let her do that in a freshly planted forest, but if we are in some bush land where there are hundreds of young wilding trees popping up in spaces that will support almost none of them it seems perfectly fine.)

I was surprised that we had to stop growing vegetables in one patch of our garden, because we used sheep pellets (i.e., sheep manure) to cultivate the

CHAPTER 6. WE LEARNED THE HARD WAY

soil, and Hazel goes crazy for them. So, we grow those vegetables only in another part of the garden instead.

I am surprised by how often and how deeply I have to wash Hazel's harness, collar and, to a lesser extent, her lead. At least once a week, I put them in a bucket of soapy water, agitate them, leave them to soak for an hour (giving tea- or coffee-colored water, depending upon her adventures), and then rinse them out. Then, I wash them again. That is, I wash them twice each time I wash them, because washing them once turned out to be insufficient. We think that the natural oils in her fur coat are part of the problem.

When walking, Hazel will suddenly lunge at something. Sometimes it is a cat I did not see, or it is a discarded chicken bone, or a cat poo she wants to eat, etc. The shearing force on my shoulders and lower spine is awful, not to mention the consequences if she actually gets ahold of what she is lunging for. I usually hold her lead in my left hand, and she walks alongside me on my right-hand side, with the lead running through my right hand. Although I work out five days a week, can easily do over 100 push-ups, can easily do over 1,000 sit ups, and can run five miles without even noticing, I am surprised that Hazel's lunging has torn something in both my shoulders, with the left being worse than the right. The problem is that she is very strong, her lunges are explosively sudden, and I am attached to her by her lead. I am surprised that some young women I see out walking have their large dog tied to a belt around their waist. Perhaps they tie them to their waists because women tend to have a lower center of gravity than men and weaker upper-body strength; personally, I would never risk that with Hazel.

Given these injuries, I now almost always hold Hazel's lead with two hands. This is aided by using a two-point harness that has a V shape where the folded lead meets the loop handle. So, I can hold the lead with my left hand and hook my right hand into the V. Then, when she lunges, I can use a (stronger) curling motion with my right arm to pull her in, instead of a weaker motion with my left arm. It helps if I turn my left hand palm upwards to enable also a stronger curling motion with my left hand. The shoulder damage has been slowly healing for a few months now, given these changes, but I wish I had known about these curling grips sooner.

I am surprised at the constant vigilance required

CHAPTER 6. WE LEARNED THE HARD WAY

when walking Hazel. She often has her nose to the ground looking for something to eat (cat poo, dog poo, possum poo, chicken bones, you name it). It is exhausting to have to watch 18 inches (45cm) in front of her snout, constantly trying to anticipate her trying to eat something. For example, as I write this, twice in the last 10 days Hazel has suddenly lunged and got a whole animal poo (cat? small dog?) in her mouth and I have had to kneel down immediately, hold her mouth open, and shake her head a little to get the poo to fall out. Both times I got poo on my hands and I had to complete the rest of the walk with hands smelling of (and smudged with) cat or dog poo; I need to be more careful.

On one recent dog walk, Hazel failed to do her poo but did snatch up and eat some other dog's poo. When I got home and mentioned this, my daughter joked that Hazel had come home with more poo inside her than when she left!

Before we got Hazel, we did not realize how bad would be her habit of lunging suddenly at things in the street and trying to eat them (e.g., dropped food, cat poo, chicken bones, etc.). Most puppy literature we read made it sound like something they outgrow. So, going forwards, we plan to introduce some new training. We plan to place some tempting things on the sidewalk outside our house, shorten her lead, and reward her for walking past them. We can start with a simple temptation, like bread crusts with peanut butter on them, and progress to something irresistible, like seaweed. We hope that during the training, she will realize that the short lead means that she cannot even get the temptation in the first place, and that she will be rewarded with high-value treats (e.g., moist chicken breast) if she walks with us right past it. The training will be a success when she knowingly walks by an irresistible treat on a typical-length lead, but it will need frequent reinforcement, perhaps best done *in situ*.

Never trust or believe any child who promises to care for any animal. Children want what they want, with no comprehension of the responsibility involved or the impact on their lives. If the animal arrives and they do not or cannot care for it, then you cannot compel them to do so in any healthy way. Do not get the animal unless *you* are prepared to care for it 95% of the time. It is analogous to co-signing a loan for a family member or friend: Do not sign unless you are prepared to assume the obligation and make the payments.

At the beach, Hazel seeks out seaweed. This means that letting her run free on the beach is

CHAPTER 6. WE LEARNED THE HARD WAY

stressful because we always have to be on the look out for seaweed. (Not to mention being on the look out for seals, sea lions, leopard seals, etc.) Seaweed tends to accumulate at the high-tide mark, and that is usually uphill from where we walk and on softer sand. Running up hill on soft sand to stop her eating seaweed is really hard physical work. If Hazel eats seaweed, she often gets sick and vomits, typically at night. Vet bills could be hundreds of dollars if it gets stuck inside her (e.g., the $550 example above). We do find that after extreme tides (especially ones driven by an ocean surge), the beaches tend to be clear of seaweed. These are good times to let her run freely.

We have a muzzle for Hazel. We have used it on occasion, including at beaches, to stop her eating seaweed. Unfortunately, she hates it. She finds it uncomfortable and constraining. She seems immediately depressed when we put her muzzle on her. How would you like to be out jogging at the park or the beach wearing a muzzle? Well, that is how Hazel feels about it too. We almost never use it now, and have not used it in the last 18 months.

Hazel likes to eat long grass. This has several consequences. Sometimes she vomits it up relatively quickly, and it is bright green odiferous vomit. Sometimes she swallows it down and does not vomit until the middle of the night. Sometimes she does not vomit, but it makes her poo long and stringy and she has trouble pushing it out. Then we have to help her by pulling it out of her bum. The longest grassy poo I have pulled out of her bum was about eight inches (20cm). Obviously, I always have a plastic bag on my hand when I do that.

At the end of summer, I want to cut the grass and leave the clippings to act as compost for the lawn. However, I know that Hazel will eat the clippings and vomit them up at 2AM. So, I cannot do it. I have to collect them all. As a consequence, my lawn is not as healthy as it could be.

We were surprised when the vet told us that Hazel needed to lose weight. She looked very fit and got lots of exercise. We argued that as an English Labrador, not an American Labrador, she had a stocky build. Nevertheless, we did monitor her food more closely, and over the course of the next six months she lost about three pounds (1.5kg). The vet was impressed. She said that most Labradors gain weight rather than losing weight. We figured that maybe the vet was right about her weight after all, which also surprised us, but we also thought she was a little too slender. So, we let her weight

CHAPTER 6. WE LEARNED THE HARD WAY

climb back part half-way to where it was, and we are keeping an eye on it.

On the weight front, we talked to another dog owner who said that she never used food to train her dog because of weight problems. We told her that we know how much food to give Hazel each day, and that we subtract from that amount a small Tupperware container's worth of dog kibble for training each day. I make a point of cutting the dime-sized kibble into halves and even quarters, to make it go further. This allows us to control her food intake very closely.

Hazel has four arch-enemy neighborhood dogs that come readily to mind. Each of them has something about them that makes them different from a plain-vanilla dog: One of them is owned by a man who has not socialized his dog at all, and he walks his dog off-lead because he has not trained it on-lead (yes, this is the one Hazel jumped on); one looks like a large long-haired German Shepard and always walks with a stoop, like a wolf; one looks like a *giant* shaggy Irish Wolf Hound; and, one is a large tall slender dog that walks oddly because of a lame foot. In each case, when Hazel sees the arch-enemy dog, she stands stock still, stares for a second or two, then rears up on her hind legs barking. We think she views these dogs as different from a typical dog, and therefore as a threat. The differences that we see include non-social behavior, large size, shaggy coat, walking with a stoop, and walking with a disability. We wonder if some of these dogs also smell differently from other dogs.

The woman who walks the stooped shaggy arch-enemy dog through our neighborhood always crosses the street when she sees us coming, never makes eye contact, never says hello, and does not look happy. I suspect that her dog is disliked by most dogs.

There are some valuable lessons here: you need to work hard to socialize your dog (with dogs and humans) unless you want other dogs being aggressive towards it; and, if you pick a dog that is very large and/or very shaggy and/or disabled, then it might be viewed as a threat by other dogs, who are then aggressive towards it.

I have had quite good success lately in stopping Hazel from being aggressive and barking at her arch-enemy dogs. I have taken two approaches. The first approach requires that I have a handful of kibble in my hand at all times when walking her. I usually see an arch-enemy dog before Hazel does (because my head is three or four feet higher

CHAPTER 6. WE LEARNED THE HARD WAY

than hers). Then, we cross the street or step into the street or step up someone's driveway. Then, when we pass or when the other dog passes us, I give Hazel treats and say "quiet puppy" and "good quiet puppy." If that appears to be about to fail, I hold her snout closed. The second approach is total avoidance, with an example discussed next.

Maybe once a week, while out walking Hazel, I spot an arch-enemy dog walking along, on the same side of the street, or the opposite side of the street. To avoid a confrontation, I often use a car parked in the street as a visual and physical shield. If the dog is on the other side of the street from us, I may need to speed up and then slow down, in order to keep Hazel and the arch-enemy dog at opposing ends of an imaginary line drawn through the center of the parked car. If the other dog is on our side of the street, I may haul Hazel out into the street, and slow down, to achieve the same outcome. Most times, Hazel is not even aware of the other dog; sometimes she smells it but does not see it, and I do my best to distract her.

Of course, none of the above approaches works if we suddenly find ourselves face to face with an arch-enemy dog, in a total surprise. For example, I was walking Hazel on a dark evening, and I turned a bend to come face to face with her largest arch-enemy dog. Hazel exploded instantly, and I had to apologize to the lady walking that giant dog for Hazel's barking and aggression, but I could not easily take any counter-action. The lady was understanding; I think she gets that a lot.

Let me finish my discussion of arch-enemy dogs on a positive note. Three of Hazel's best ever dog friends (Otis, Chewy, and Daisy) started out as aggressive barking yard dogs. For several months, Hazel was barked at whenever we passed their house/property and they were off-lead in the front yard or outside. I decided to counter their aggression by consistently giving them each treats. Within a few weeks, these yummy bribes transformed all three of them into welcoming and happy dog best friends to Hazel. It worked in these cases because the dogs were food-driven and off-lead with no owner in sight. However, I have not yet been able to use the same tactic with on-lead owner-accompanied arch-enemy encounters in the street, which are much more violent.

Chapter 7

Dog Ownership Pros & Cons

Let me summarize what I see as the main pros and cons of owning a dog.

7.1 Pros of Dog Ownership

- My wife and daughter can go for a walk by themselves with our big dog and be much safer than without a dog. This is not obviously true with a small dog that could easily be kicked away.

- My house is safer with a big dog on the property

CHAPTER 7. DOG OWNERSHIP PROS & CONS

than with no dog. Hazel barks at unexpected arrivals, letting them know that she is on duty. I am happy to answer the door to strangers when holding Hazel by the collar, or squeezed between my knees, because I can let her go in an instant. Hazel can frighten visitors, but I keep a 30-pound (15kg) bag of dog food on the front porch, with a picture of a German Shepard on it, along with dog toys, to warn people that we have a dog. So, it should be no surprise. I do not have a sign on the front garden gate, but I do have signs on gates to the left and right of my house.

- Other people (especially the elderly, the very young, university students away from home who miss their dogs, people in hospital, people who recently lost a dog, and people with emotional problems) get a lot of joy out of patting Hazel. This may depend upon the breed (a cute empathetic purebred Chocolate Labrador in Hazel's case). It is nice to make those people happy. I see the benefit that they get. After seeing dozens of different breeds and mixes of breeds I think that the "other people" benefit really only comes if you have a Labrador, Golden Retriever, or a Beagle. I do not see people going up to any other breeds to give them a pat.

- If you are socially awkward (e.g., autistic, introverted, etc.), or seeking a romantic partner, a well-trained attractive pure-bred dog can be an amazing ice breaker.

- Walking a dog may motivate some family members to exercise.

7.2 Cons of Dog Ownership

- The first few months of puppy ownership are intense, with constant sleep deprivation. The intense training of the first 12 months is draining.

- If you are a fit and healthy person who exercises a lot already, then please understand that adding a dog means that you *must* walk that dog. You may find that after walking the dog for an hour, and not really getting a cardio workout, your legs are too tired for your five-mile (eight-kilometer) run. Or, equivalently, after going for a run, walking the dog means that your leg muscles do not have the rest they need to recover fully from your run. Without the cardio exercise or without the recovery time, you may find that your strength and fitness *decline* after getting a dog.

CHAPTER 7. DOG OWNERSHIP PROS & CONS

- Your dog will damage more things than you thought possible: your precious garden plants, your grass, your furniture, your carpets, your electrical equipment, your wiring, your car, your wrists, your elbows, your shoulders, your lower back, your knees, and your hearing (when she lets out a bark in a small room). Your dog will steal any food left unattended and within reach. Unhappy or curious dogs can also chew on shoes, soap, cosmetics, etc.

- Your dog gets dirty, and smells like an animal. You will have fur and dog smells in your house. Your dog will vomit in the house on a regular basis. (As a puppy, it will pee, poo, and puke left, right, and center.) You have to handle dog poo all the time; it smells bad and is full of bacteria, viruses, parasites and other harmful pathogens. "Fish-butt Friday" is disgusting!

- Every day, I worry that Hazel will have a violent confrontation. Will another dog attack her with no cause? Will Hazel be aggressive to one of her arch-enemies? Will Hazel be triggered by an unusual human? Could she bite a child who acts unpredictably? It is stressful.

- Every day, we worry about Hazel eating things

7.2. CONS OF DOG OWNERSHIP

she is not supposed to eat: seaweed, discarded chicken bones, other animals' poos, cosmetics, etc. The constant vigilance required to avoid these dangers is tiring.

- After meeting 100+ dogs walking in the street and the park, I have noticed that many people walking dogs are not their owners, but friends, neighbors, workmates, relatives, and paid dog walkers. Why is that? The reason is that many people nowadays live busy lives and do not have the time to give their dog the attention it needs. If you work all day, what is that poor dog going to do? It may be at home whining, barking, and lonely. What's the point of owning a dog if your dog is in distress for half the day time?

- A dog is an expensive luxury. The direct costs can run into the thousands of dollars every year. Some costs you can budget for, like a $120 30-pound (15kg) bag of dog food every seven weeks, but some costs are a big surprise, like a $550 vet bill for seaweed stuck in the gut, or a $300 doctor's bill for examining the shoulder that your dog damaged. The indirect opportunity costs are even higher.

- Finally, for me personally, the single biggest neg-

CHAPTER 7. DOG OWNERSHIP PROS & CONS

ative of dog ownership is that dog ownership destroys personal degrees of freedom. Previously, you were free to take a trip, or be out of the house for many hours, etc., without much forethought, but not now. You were free to work a full uninterrupted day from home, but not now. You were free to sleep an extra hour on a weekend previously, but not now. You were free to choose when and whether to go for a walk, but not now; even if it is freezing cold or pouring rain, your dog still needs to get out. If an emergency comes up (e.g., rushing a child to the hospital), who cares for, walks, and feeds the dog? If you get sick and are bedridden, who cares for, walks and feeds your dog? Rain or shine, in sickness or in good health, for richer or for poorer, you are locked into walking the dog, feeding the dog, washing the dog, playing with the dog, fighting off other aggressive dogs, protecting others from your dog, bringing the dog to the vet for vaccines, etc. The bottom line is that if you look at your lifestyle and think that there is a degrees of freedom gap that is just the right size to fit a dog, be aware that once that dog arrives, you may have no degrees of freedom left at all. Owning a dog is a big responsibility, and you will need to juggle the dog's needs the way you juggle a child's needs, or you will be a frustrated owner of an unhappy dog.

7.3 Dog Ownership Checklist

- Do you (or someone in your household) have 90 minutes of free time a day to walk your dog? You may need to allow more time for some breeds, but less for others.

- Are you physically fit enough (or will you be fit enough soon) to be able to walk your dog that long?

- Are you physically strong enough (i.e., upper body and legs) to handle a large dog? If not, you may need to downsize your plans.

- Have you budgeted for the costs? Do you need insurance, or a sinking fund at the bank? (A sinking fund is a targeted savings account that you regularly deposit money into with a specific goal. For example, we put money into an account every month for five years before buying our new used car.)

- Is your house big enough for your dog to run around in when it is pouring rain outside?

- Are you prepared to protect everything in sight in your house and garden? Dogs like to bite, gnaw, chew and dig anything they can get their paws on.

- Are you prepared to have a dirty house, with pee, poo, and puke, tufts of fur, and a dog smell? You cannot have nice things and a big dog; it just does not work.

7.4 Final Words 🐾

Bringing a dog into your family is a big responsibility. Nurturing a happy dog takes lots of time, effort, and money. So, if you are busy, self-centered, or financially strained, then you should seriously reconsider whether bringing a dog into your life makes sense. We see many poorly trained dogs and many frustrated dog owners, and we do not want these outcomes for you.

Educate yourself, and spend time with friends' dogs, taking them on walks and caring for them. Once you get a good feel for what life with a dog really feels like, you will be able to make a well-

7.4. FINAL WORDS 🐾

considered educated choice about whether to add a dog to your family, and if so, which breed.

Although the above-mentioned cons of dog ownership outnumber the pros of dog ownership, Hazel the Chocolate Labrador has enriched our family life in ways we never expected. My family and I wish you the best of success in your own first-dog adventure.

References

BLS, 2025, "Economic News Release: Table B-3. Average hourly and weekly earnings of all employees on private nonfarm payrolls by industry sector, seasonally adjusted," Available at: https://www.bls.gov/news.release/empsit.t19.htm (downloaded July 23, 2025).

DOL, 2025, "Minimum Wage," Available at: https://www.dol.gov/general/topic/wages/minimumwage (downloaded July 23, 2025).

Hart, Benjamin L., Lynette A. Hart, Abigail P. Thigpen, and Neil H. Willits, 2020, "Assisting Decision-Making on Age of Neutering for 35 Breeds of Dogs: Associated Joint Disorders, Cancers, and Urinary Incontinence," *Frontiers in Veterinary Science*, Vol. 7, (July), Discussed at: https://www.ucdavis.edu/news/when-should-you-neuter-your-dog-avoid-health-risks, Available at: https://www.frontiersin.org/journals/

REFERENCES

veterinary-science/articles/10.3389/fvets.2020.00388/full.

Hart, Lynette A., Abigail P. Thigpen, Benjamin L. Hart, Neil H. Willits, Maya Lee, Miya M. Babchuk, Jenna Lee, Megan Ho, Sara T. Clarkson, and Juliann W. Chou, 2024, "Assisting Decision-making on Age of Neutering for German Short/Wirehaired Pointer, Mastiff, Newfoundland, Rhodesian Ridgeback, Siberian Husky: Associated Joint Disorders, Cancers, and Urinary Incontinence," *Frontiers in Veterinary Science*, Vol. 12 (April), Discussed at: https://www.ucdavis.edu/health/news/when-should-you-neuter-or-spay-your-dog, Available at: https://www.frontiersin.org/journals/veterinary-science/articles/10.3389/fvets.2024.1322276/full.

Rao, Sunaina, 2021, "How Dogs and Humans See The World Differently: Dogs Have Contrasting Visual Abilities When Compared to Humans," Available at: https://fromtbot.com/life/do-dogs-see-like-humans/ (dated August 17, 2021; downloaded June 1, 2025).

Index

𝒜
Abigail P. Thigpen, 146
anal glands, 31–34
apples, 53
arch-enemies, 130–133
assumed male, 66
attacks, 51–53, 113–117

ℬ
Babchuk, Miya M., 146
bath, 81
biting, 68
blood, 57
BLS, 20, 145
bored, 117
breeds, 4–6, 14
broken glass, 47
brushes and combs, 81

𝒞
car seat belt, 47
car seat cover, 54
cats and rabbits, 86
chick magnet, 85
Chou, Juliann W., 146
Clarkson, Sara T., 146
coffee, 40
commands, 10–13
    do nothing, 13
condolences, 62–64
confusion, 89
costs, 16–20
    opportunity, 19
crate training, 119
cushions, 98

𝒟
dandruff, 82
day care, 27
deodorant, 112
depth perception, 119
dog sitter, 37
doggles, 73
DOL, 20, 145
dreams, 94
dyskinesia, 94–97

INDEX

ℰ
exercise, 7–9, 28–29

ℱ
face-planting, 118
fetch, 113
FRAP, 71

𝒢
genetics, 65
gestation period, 36
grass, 128
grass seed, 39
growls, 75
guide dogs, 86

ℋ
happy tail syndrome, 112
Hart, Benjamin L., 15, 16, 145, 146
Hart, Lynette A., 15, 145, 146
Hazel hug, 69
heart rhythm, 97
Henry's pocket, 87
high-vis Hazel, 66
Ho, Megan, 146
hospital visits, 101–104
hunting, 79

ℐ
injuries, 54–56

𝒥
jumping up, 68

𝒦
kennel, 37–38
kitchen, 97
Kong, 92

ℒ
Labrador flop, 105–107
leads crossed, 109
Lee, Jenna, 146
Lee, Maya, 146
lip balm, 40
long lead, 44
lunging, 124–127

ℳ
missing eye, 46
money, 16–20
mush mush, 93
muzzle, 128

𝒪
oven controls, 110

𝒫
pigeons, 100
play dates, 118
poisons, 30
poo bags, 108
prickles, 38
pros and cons, 135
public property, 82
puppy classes, 10

INDEX

Q
quiet puppy, 13, 121

R
Rao, Sunaina, 146
REM sleep, 93
rescue dog, 7, 104

S
scent trail, 61–62
sea lion, 46
seasonal moods, 87–88
seaweed, 36, 127
sleep deprivation, 24
soap, 111
spaying/neutering, 15–16
sugar face, 87
Sunday drivers, 41
support network, 20
swimming lesson, 35

T
teeth, 78, 121–123
Thigpen, Abigail P., 145
Tom and Jerry, 76
Total Recall, 10
two-point harness, 109–110

V
vision, 101

W
wasp sting, 39

Web sites
    Amazon.com, viii, 150–156
    TheLabradorSite.com, 10
weight, 129–130
Willits, Neil H., 145, 146
wrong car, 75

Z
zoomies, 71

24 Essential Tips for Selling
Print Replica eBooks on Amazon:
How to Capture New Readers by Turning
Your Physical Book into an eBook
Timothy Falcon Crack

*PhD (MIT), MCom, PGDipCom,
BSc (HONS 1st Class), IMC*

This 54-page eBook gives more than two-dozen essential tips accumulated over years of turning self-published physical print books into "print replica" eBooks sold on www.Amazon.com. (What did I learn the hard way? What did I wish I had known before I published eBooks? What are the biggest trip-ups you need to watch out for?) A print replica eBook uses a simple pdf-formatted text block. So, there is no messing around with unfamiliar EPUB or MOBI formatting, HTML code, or reflowable eBooks (i.e., where the book reorganizes itself when the reader resizes the text). If you are not selling your books as eBooks, then you are missing out on customers and the royalty income they provide!

---

www.Amazon.com (Kindle)
timcrack@alum.mit.edu

How to Ace Your Business Finance Class: Essential Knowledge and Techniques to Master the Material and Ace Your Exams
Timothy Falcon Crack
PhD (MIT), MCom, PGDipCom, BSc (HONS 1st Class), IMC

A pocket-sized book for students (or instructors) in a first university finance class. I use 25 years experience teaching this material to explain carefully the stumbling blocks that consistently trip up students. Chapters titles: Foundations, Financial Statements, TVM I (One Cash Flow), TVM II (Multiple Cash Flows), Inflation and Indices, Bonds and Interest Rates, Equities and Dividend Discount Models, Capital Budgeting I (Decision Rules), Capital Budgeting II (Cash Flows), Capital Budgeting III (Cost of Capital), Capital Budgeting IV (A Paradox), The CAPM and Interest Rates, Risk and Return, Market Efficiency, Capital Structure, and Dividends.

---

www.Amazon.com (Paperback)
www.Amazon.com (Kindle)
timcrack@alum.mit.edu

Heard on The Street:
Quantitative Questions from Wall Street Job Interviews
Timothy Falcon Crack

PhD (MIT), MCom, PGDipCom, BSc (HONS 1st Class), IMC

A must read! Over 240 quant questions collected from actual job interviews in investment banking, investment management, and options trading. The interviewers use the same questions year-after-year, and here they are—with solutions! These questions come from all types of interviews (corp. finance, sales and trading, quant research, etc.). The questions come from all levels of interviews (undergrad, MS, MBA, PhD). The latest edition also includes 260+ non-quant actual interview questions, and a revised section on interview technique. Questions from **traditional corporate finance** interviews are indicated with a bank symbol in the margin (72 of the quant questions and 196 of the non-quant questions).

---

www.Amazon.com (Paperback)
www.Amazon.com (Kindle)
timcrack@alum.mit.edu

Pocket Heard on The Street
Timothy Falcon Crack

PhD (MIT), MCom, PGDipCom, BSc (HONS 1st Class), IMC

These two pocket-sized editions fit in your pocket or purse, and are easy to read on the subway, bus, train, or plane! They are a carefully curated selection of the best questions from the full-sized edition of *Heard on The Street*. The red covered edition has 75 quant questions, with detailed solutions. The yellow-covered edition has 20 brain teasers, 30 thinking questions, and over 100 non-quantitative questions. The brain teasers, and more than half the thinking questions have detailed solutions. The quant questions in the red edition usually require math/stats, but the brain teasers and "thinking questions" in the yellow edition usually require little or no math; the thinking questions are in between.

---

www.Amazon.com (Paperback)
www.Amazon.com (Kindle)
timcrack@alum.mit.edu

Basic Black-Scholes:
Option Pricing and Trading
Timothy Falcon Crack

*PhD (MIT), MCom, PGDipCom,
BSc (HONS 1st Class), IMC*

Extremely clear explanations of Black-Scholes option pricing theory, and applications of theory to trading. Based on award-winning teaching at Indiana University. The presentation does not go far beyond basic Black-Scholes because a novice need not go far beyond Black-Scholes to make money, all high-level option pricing theory extends Black-Scholes, and other books go far beyond Black-Scholes without the firm foundations given here. Includes Bloomberg screens, expanded analysis of Black-Scholes interpretations, and downloadable spreadsheets to forecast profits and transactions costs, and to explore option sensitivities (the Greeks).

---

www.Amazon.com (Paperback)
www.Amazon.com (Kindle)
timcrack@alum.mit.edu

Foundations for Scientific Investing:
Capital Markets Intuition and
Critical Thinking Skills
Timothy Falcon Crack

*PhD (MIT), MCom, PGDipCom,
BSc (HONS 1st Class), IMC*

A firm foundation for thinking about and conducting investment. It helps to build capital markets intuition and critical thinking skills. Every investor needs these skills to conduct confident, deliberate, and skeptical investment. This book is the product of 25 years of investment research and experience (academic, personal, and professional) and 20+ painstaking years of destructive testing in university classrooms. The integration of finance, economics, accounting, pure mathematics, statistics, numerical techniques, and spreadsheets (or programming) make this an ideal capstone course at the advanced undergraduate or masters/MBA level.

---

www.Amazon.com (Paperback)
www.Amazon.com (Kindle)
timcrack@alum.mit.edu

Foundations for Scientific Investing: Multiple-Choice, Short Answer, and Long-Answer Test Questions
Timothy Falcon Crack
PhD (MIT), MCom, PGDipCom, BSc (HONS 1st Class), IMC

This book accompanies *Foundations for Scientific Investing*. It provides 700+ class-tested questions (600+ multiple-choice questions and 125 short-answer questions), plus the long-answer questions already appearing in *Foundations for Scientific Investing*). Suggested solutions to the multiple-choice and short-answer questions are given. The multiple-choice questions may also be useful as a test bank for instructors in any advanced investments class.

```
www.Amazon.com (Paperback)
www.Amazon.com (Kindle)
timcrack@alum.mit.edu
```

PUBREF:20250802:15:01.200,718.OU

www.ingramcontent.com/pod-product-compliance
Lightning Source LLC
LaVergne TN
LVHW051602070426
835507LV00021B/2715